67

Ways to Protect
Seniors from
Crime

❖ ❖ ❖

J. L. Simmons, Ph.D.

An Owl Book
Henry Holt and Company   New York

Henry Holt and Company, Inc.
Publishers since 1866
115 West 18th Street
New York, New York 10011

Henry Holt® is a registered
trademark of Henry Holt and Company, Inc.

Library of Congress Cataloging-in-Publication Data
Simmons, J. L. (Jerry Laird).
67 ways to protect seniors from crime/J. L. Simmons.—1st Owl book ed.
p.   cm.
Includes bibliographical references.
1. Aged—United States—Crimes against.   2. Crime prevention—United
States.   I. Title.   II. Title: Sixty-seven ways to protect seniors from crime.
HV6250.4.A34S56   1993
362.88'084'6—dc20   92-43408
                                                                CIP

ISBN 0-8050-2496-4 (An Owl Book: pbk.)

First Owl Book Edition—1993

DESIGNED BY PAULA R. SZAFRANSKI

Printed in the United States of America
All first editions are printed on acid-free paper.∞

1   3   5   7   9   10   8   6   4   2

Important Notice:
Every effort has been made to provide accurate information and effective crime prevention tactics, but no guarantees of safety can be made by the author or publisher. Responsibility for the use of the advice in this book rests solely with the reader. For medical or legal questions, consult with a licensed health professional or an attorney.

In many cultures throughout the world, seniors are regarded as "treasures of the tribe." They are looked up to for guidance in all matters: practical, emotional, and spiritual.

Seniors are the elders of our tribe—and our world now sorely needs their knowledge, experience, and wisdom. They deserve better than they sometimes get.

This book may help save a few seniors' lives and save a few thousand seniors from being victimized or impoverished, so it is a labor of love.

Contents

THREE

FOUR

FIVE

Acknowledgments

I am indebted and grateful to the many people who made contributions to this book.

First, I would like to gratefully acknowledge the help of Nola Simmons, my sweet wife and partner. Indeed, her efforts add up to a full collaboration—coauthorship.

Theresa Burns, my editor at Henry Holt, has steadfastly performed the twin roles of inspiring guru and drill instructor, and the book is far better because of it.

My colleague Dr. George J. McCall made numerous contributions, for which I warmly thank him.

I would also like to acknowledge my agents, Michael Larsen and Elizabeth Pomada, for all their efforts in my behalf.

Thanks also to Lisa Goldberg, production editor, and to Ruth Flaxman, copy editor, for their diligent work on the book, and to Ruth Weiner, publicist, for helping spread the word.

There is, finally, my gratitude to all of the older people from whom I've learned so much down through the years—

my grandmother, "Gammy"; many of my teachers; my mother-in-law, Edna Cox; scores of senior clients, students, and research respondents; and most of my current friends and relatives. Their contributions are on every page of this book.

Introduction:
The Bad News and
Good News About
Seniors and Crime

When I was a kid we didn't lock our doors. I could go walking in the park alone or go swimming at midnight or try out clumsy kisses in lovers' lane with no more risk than my parents finding out. Those are bygone days.

Today, as if we seniors don't have enough concerns, we are increasingly haunted by the specter of crime. In a nationwide survey, the Figgie Foundation found that 70 percent of those questioned expressed a fear of crime, and that women and older people were the most fearful.

These fears are not just imaginary. The federal government's Bureau of Justice Statistics estimates that one out of every four households is touched in some way by serious crime each year. And although many seniors have never been personally mugged or burglarized or swindled, they surely know people who have.

Nobody wants to be a victim of crime, yet too many seniors

are. We hear about a seventy-year-old woman being pushed into her apartment, robbed, and raped. An old friend's purse is stolen at the mall. A famous elderly newspaper columnist reports how he was struck and robbed on his way to the parking lot. A sixty-eight-year-old TV talk show guest tells how she was bilked out of her life savings. And magazine articles warn seniors about street violence, the corruption of corporations, the dangers of quacks, and the malpractice of some doctors. So it's easy to become anxious about our own personal safety.

The famous 1968 President's Task Force on Victims of Crime's final report concluded: "Every citizen of this country is impoverished, less free, more fearful and less safe, because of the ever-present fear of criminals."

There is more crime victimization of seniors today because (1) there is more crime and (2) there are more seniors than ever before. Exact figures are hard to get, but everyone agrees that crime rates have dramatically risen over the last three decades. And, in all modern industrial countries, there are now more people over sixty than teenagers, according to United Nations census data.

Risks of many kinds of crime drop off sharply after age thirty, Federal Bureau of Investigation (FBI) statistics indicate. Yet older people are still sometimes vulnerable to street assaults, burglary, and even rape. And the risk of being swindled actually increases—seniors have more accumulated resources than any other age group and the schemers know this well.

The good news is that at least nine out of ten crimes can be prevented if we take simple protective measures. It might seem that crime happens randomly, but it doesn't. There are always circumstances that make crime possible. But other circumstances can prevent crime from happening. Criminals, like viruses, are always around—it's our preventive actions that make the difference.

Statisticians talk of "average risks," but actually there are almost no "average persons." A senior's (or anyone's) personal crime risks are virtually always much less or much greater than these averages. The average risk of being burglarized, for instance, in a neighborhood might be 1 in 40, but if someone is careless, their risk might be 1 in 5. Yet, one FBI study estimates that if someone follows many of the measures outlined in this book, the risk might drop to 1 in 600. Criminals are opportunists, so all we need to do is take steps to curtail their opportunities.

This book will show you how to avoid becoming a crime victim. It contains hundreds of easy-to-apply tips for crime-proofing the rest of your life. In keeping with our uncertain economic times, most of these techniques cost little or nothing.

Because we are dealing with the vagaries of life, there can be no 100 percent guarantees. But whatever your living arrangements, they can be made more secure; whatever your lifestyle, it can be made more crime-free. Each security step you take will shift the odds further in your favor.

The data and tactics on the following pages are drawn from criminology research, the recommendations of veteran crime-prevention workers and victim counselors, in-depth studies of criminals themselves, and my own extensive professional work in the area.

Being a senior is a "life stage" thing—its opportunities and concerns are qualitatively different from those of other life stages. And crime is different for seniors.

I began my studies of older people when, as a fair-haired

young graduate student, I worked on the 1962 White House Conference on Aging. Soon after, I began studying crime and publishing articles on deviance and the start of the drug-use epidemic. As the next three decades passed, I taught in several universities, did a heap of research, and wrote a double-handful of books—the last one being *76 Ways to Protect Your Child from Crime*. Now that my hair has grayed, it seems appropriate that I bring these two subjects of crime and aging together in the book you're holding.

I, my wife, and the majority of our friends and relatives are "senior citizens." We've heard the jokes, sweated over the concerns, and shrugged off the minor pains, too. I don't have the answers to the big questions about being older, but I can help you stay crime-free.

❖ ONE ❖

The Who, What, Where, When, and Why of Crime

Protecting ourselves from crime boils down to two things: recognizing what the hazards are and eliminating or thwarting these risks. We can do these two things better if we know what we're up against. The actual current crime situation is somewhat different from the picture we are given by the media and our politicians.

The entries in this first chapter sketch some "know your enemy" fundamentals that can help you thwart the bad guys.

#1

False Myths About Aging That Can Lead to Crime

Any victimization, exploitation, or discrimination against seniors is a crime. Yet false myths about aging aid and abet such ill-treatment in countless direct and subtle ways.

In many societies young people were considered apprentices in the business of living, adults were the journeymen, and older persons were the masters. But negative stereotypes about seniors have in recent decades been prevalent in some industrial countries. As sociologist James Henslin wrote: "Old age came to be seen as a disorder for which there was no cure," while youth's attributes came to be idolized.

Massive scientific evidence has now proven these negative stereotypes to be false. Yet they still linger like shadows across the lives of older people. These false myths create two main problems for everyone. First, older people sometimes are themselves taken in by these myths to such an extent that they become self-fulfilling. For example, *everyone* forgets phone numbers, but seniors who do so will sometimes worry that their minds are deteriorating. Second, the myths can be used to criminally abuse older people in some manner, such as overmedicating them or "managing" their finances.

One of the most frequent complaints I hear from seniors is that younger people—doctors, nurses, social workers, even relatives—haven't a clue about what it means to be older and act instead on the basis of these false myths. More and more older people are becoming "mad as hell" about this and are demanding fair and realistic treatment.

So let's compare the myths with the facts.

FALSE MYTH: Seniors are mostly useless and a burden on society.

FACT: Older people mostly keep the world running. They comprise most of the world's business, cultural, and political leaders. They call most of the shots in most public and private organizations, at both the global and the local levels. Far from being has-beens, they are at the forefront of world civilization.

FALSE MYTH: Seniors are less creative and poor workers.

FACT: The majority of the *New York Times* best-sellers are written by older people. And the U.S. Department of Labor has found that older workers have less absenteeism, fewer on-the-job accidents, lower turnover rates, and equivalent efficiency with younger workers. Younger workers consistently have more sick days per year than seniors.

Physiological studies find that there is only a 2 percent decline per decade in the speed of nerve impulse transmission in the older body, and this is more than made up for by increased discernment and judgment. A corporation executive told me, "Older workers are a tad slower, but they make fewer errors and wiser judgments. They don't hit the wrong buttons." So there really is no legitimate basis for job discrimination.

FALSE MYTH: Intelligence declines as one gets older.

FACT: On untimed mental ability tests, the majority of people maintain or improve mental performance as they grow older, even after age eighty. Only 5 percent show serious mental impairment—a percentage not all that much higher than the general population. Gerontologist Ken Dychtwald has pointed out, "The healthy aged brain is as active and efficient as the healthy young brain."

There is growing evidence that inductive abilities—the ability to distill bottom lines and synthesize large masses of data—*improves* as one grows older. For example, the number of connecting linkages between brain cells seems to increase. Perhaps this is the source of the wisdom that has traditionally been attributed to age.

FALSE MYTH: Seniors have trouble managing their own affairs, drift into second childhood, and become senile.

FACT: "Senility" affects only a small fraction of even the very elderly. Many alleged cases of senility turn out upon expert medical examination to be malnutrition or other conditions that can be remedied. In public nursing homes apparent senility cases often result from overmedication. So there is usually no justification for taking away their rights through such maneuvers as "guardianships."

FALSE MYTH: Seniors are usually financially impoverished.

FACT: There are some older people below the poverty line. Yet, on average, they have more discretionary income than any other age group. Older persons aid younger relatives financially four times as often as youngsters help elder relatives. Those over fifty make up one-quarter of our total population, but they own over three-fourths of all the financial assets. This is why swindlers swarm around them.

FALSE MYTH: Most seniors are frail and in chronic ill health.

FACT: Only around 20 percent are debilitated by health problems—at most, twice the rate for the general population. They have some aches and pains, but then almost everyone does. Most seniors report feeling quite well usually. Only 5 percent are in nursing homes. In a Commonwealth Fund survey, over half of those seventy-five and older declared themselves to be in excellent or good health. The very real medical complaints of seniors, especially women, are, however, sometimes dismissed as "just old age." (My mother-in-law has gotten this "treatment" several times.) And they are sometimes victimized by unnecessary surgeries and health care scams.

FALSE MYTH: Seniors are over the hill romantically and sexually.

FACT: The majority, surveys show, remain romantically interested and sexually active. As with all other age groups, there's a great deal of variation in sexual activity and interest, yet many seniors report their lovemaking is better than it used to be, and a third report that they enjoy experimentation. But this continuing interest can leave them vulnerable to "charming" swindlers, as we'll see.

FALSE MYTH: Seniors are set in their ways and conformist, and they shun the new.

FACT: Teenagers conform the most to social peer pressure and older people the least. Many seniors start new businesses and careers, get advanced degrees, get in shape physically, become celebrities, plunge into whirlwind romances, and recover from major illnesses and traumas.

I spoke with a marketing expert who said that marketers didn't target older people very much because they were inflexible. When I probed deeper, he finally admitted that the problem was *seniors were less suggestible to persuasion.*

FALSE MYTH: Seniors are a sad and lonely lot.

FACT: Some are. But no age group has a monopoly on loneliness or depression. A nationwide *Los Angeles Times* poll found that nearly two-thirds of those over sixty-five said they were pleased with their personal lives. And a National Opinion Research Center study recently found that people over sixty-five were on average the *happiest* age group.

I've casually asked a number of older people: "Would you like to be twenty again?" Some said yes, but only if they could keep their current knowledge and resources too. Others said, "I'd love to." And some said something like, "Hell, no! I was miserable and crazy as a loon at that age."

Negative myths like these are fading now as the true evidence accumulates and as seniors provide living proof that these myths are false. But the stereotypes are still far too often held by family, acquaintances, health care professionals—and criminals. One way or another, negative myths are used against us.

The older years are qualitatively different from other life stages, but not lesser. It would seem that increased intergenerational tolerance and understanding would benefit everyone except the victimizers and exploiters. In a commencement address at American University, President John F. Kennedy remarked, "If we cannot end our differences, at least we can help make the world safe for diversity."

#2

Changing Times, Changing Crimes

The fact that times have changed is no news to seniors. After all, we've lived through these changes and have had an active hand in bringing many of them about. Whether the world is going to hell in a handcart or poised on the brink of a brighter day, we've "paid our dues."

Yet no one can keep abreast of everything that is going on. Unless you work directly in crime prevention, it's hard to separate the true current crime scene from the distorted and sensationalized media coverage. And so much about the conditions and crime risks for seniors has changed from even a generation ago. It's important to know about these changes so you can more effectively protect yourself.

The present older generation is, on the average, healthier, more active, smarter, sexier, and more long-lived than previous senior generations. As a group, we have more discretionary income to spend as we please, we have more mobility, and there are more of us. There have been baby booms before, but never before has there been a senior boom. So both the world and we have changed.

Criminals have changed too. One of my aims is to give you

more of the facts about the current crop of crooks so you know who and what you're dealing with.

Here are a few of the broad crime changes that have happened in recent years.

* *There are more criminals than there used to be.* No one really knows why, and we can't get exact, reliable figures. But the number of arrests for every type of crime has risen significantly in the last thirty years, according to official FBI statistics. Teenagers, adults, and even the elderly, are committing more crimes—from the ghettos to the corporate boardrooms. So to be secure, we need to use more savvy and alertness, in the same way we must be more alert driving in unpleasant weather.

* *Today's criminals tend to be more violent.* The brilliant criminologist Marvin Wolfgang followed the criminal careers of thousands of men, during two different time periods, as they grew from birth into adulthood. His massive data shows that, without question, today's law-breakers have become more mean, nasty, and vicious in their doings. (The drug epidemic may be part of the reason, along with the coddling of serious repeat juvenile offenders.)

  This increase in nastiness has been taken into account in the pages that follow. The essential point is to regard today's criminals warily, as wild animals who may be unpredictable, irrational, and under little self-control. For this reason, don't call them punks or argue with them.

* *Today's crime problems are less under control by law enforcement agencies.* Despite their heroic efforts, the

police and regulatory officials are less able to keep our streets and homes secure. As one symptom of this, our courts and prisons are so overcrowded that culprits are sometimes set free again with little more than a slap on the wrist. So personal crime protection is, more than ever, in our own hands. Luckily, our own actions can make the difference.

+ *Consumer frauds, scams, and corporate crimes are on the rise.* According to one U.S. Department of Justice estimate, these cost our society eighteen times as much as all street crimes combined. Modern societies are only beginning to come to grips with this problem; meanwhile, we need to hold on to our wallets and be our own watchdogs.

+ *Good news—a lot more is now known about how criminals operate.* Thanks to the dedicated work of a legion of crime researchers, we now know a lot more about how criminals think and what they look for—also, who gets hit, robbed, burglarized, or swindled, and who doesn't. These research findings can be translated into effective crime-protection tactics, and that's what I've done. Most tactics are as simple as slipping on a coat in cold weather. And even if you run into an erupting civil disturbance, like the Los Angeles riots, your risks can be minimized.

In a more perfect world, we should just be free to go where we want, leave our doors unlocked, and greet all strangers with a smile. Unfortunately, we don't now live in such a world, so we have to be prudent.

There's an old Spanish saying, "If you want good service, serve yourself," and that is the heart of personal security.

#3

Who Are the Criminals?

A few years back, when I taught university courses at a state prison, I became acquainted with dozens of convicted felons. I would talk with them during the break about politics, music, the weather, and their families, to the point where I'd almost forget who I was talking to. One resembled the grocer at our local market. Another looked and behaved like our accountant. Some struggled with the course materials while others sailed right through. And they seemed no more threatening than my students at the local university. Yet, sitting before me were murderers, brutal spouse abusers, dope dealers, career burglars, and merciless swindlers. My colleague who taught at the women's state prison reported similar experiences. I learned some lessons.

How can you spot a criminal? You can't. Unfortunately, the villains don't wear identifying black hats for our convenience. In fact, the majority of them take great pains to blend in and pass for law-abiding citizens.

Despite two centuries of effort, researchers have uncovered no "criminal type" or "criminal mind." A scruffy long-haired youth passing you on the street isn't necessarily dangerous, and a well-dressed older woman knocking on your front door isn't necessarily safe. You can't judge by looks or stereotypes alone. I've known of a great many cases where seniors were fooled, then victimized, by appearances, so this is vital to keep in mind.

Street crimes—robberies, rapes, burglaries, and violence—are mostly a young person's game. U.S. Department of Justice figures show that seven out of eight persons arrested for such felonies are under thirty-five, while those over sixty-five account for only 1 percent of arrests. Over four out of every five street crimes are committed by males, although female crime rates have been rising too. Grab-and-run thieves can be of any age, including small children. And swindlers tend to be older than street hoodlums. These rate differences are only tendencies, but you are surely much safer in senior centers than on inner-city streets.

There are roughly three types of street criminals. First, there are the real professionals, who are extremely cunning yet very seldom violent. They are highly skilled and can outwit almost any defense system. But they go after big game—banks, businesses, and the rich—and they almost never bother with the rest of us.

Second are the habitual criminals who aren't pros but are chronic lawbreakers. They know a few tricks of the trade and may commit dozens of crimes before being brought down by the authorities. Many of the tactics on the following pages are designed to help you avoid or thwart them.

By far the largest number of street criminals are amateurs, but luckily, these are the easiest to deter. They are impulsive and opportunistic and easily discouraged by simple security measures. They are usually young and naive about the world, but they can easily become vicious, so don't try to lecture or reform them on your own.

Researcher Yves Brillon studied the data from the United States, Canada, and England and found that older people are the least likely age group to be the victims of robbers, rapists, burglars, or the violent. There seem to be two good reasons for such reduced risks: (1) Most seniors have a less crime-prone lifestyle and (2) they have much more savvy in the ways of the world. Older people usually aren't as fleet-footed as youths but this is more than made up for by the fact that they have more hard-won sense. As the saying goes, they weren't born yesterday.

The biggest threats to seniors are the legions of frauds, scams, ripoffs, and financial exploitations aimed at us these days. Better Business Bureaus, federal agencies, and state attorney general offices are now flooded with cases of such crimes—more than they can even begin to deal with. It's as if somebody declared open season on us. And again, we can't rely on appearances. Swindles can come from acquaintances, blue-chip companies, or trusted professionals, as well as heartless con artists.

Criminals are not nice people; they are parasites and about as glamorous as doggie-do. They operate on the profit motive. In a sense they are the ultimate ruthless capitalists, who seek to maximize their profits with as little cost as possible and with no human compassion for their "customers."

Happily, the criminals are still a minority—there are a lot more of us than there are of them.

#4

Five Leading Crime-Risk Factors

There are high-risk factors in crime victimization, just as there are high-risk factors that can endanger your health. The following factors greatly increase a senior's crime risks above the normal odds because they play right into the hands of the bad guys.

1. ***Failing to close and lock up.*** Yes, we've all done it. But as many as half of all types of thefts and one-fifth of all crimes against persons result from neglecting to lock entrances, windows, and *all* car doors and not securing valuables under lock and key. Closing and locking won't stop a determined pro. But most amateurs lack either the time or the skill to breach a half-decent barrier, even a closed purse flap. The days when we could leave our doors and bikes and cars unlocked are now long gone.

2. ***Being in the wrong place at the wrong time.*** I've studied hundreds of newspaper stories about local crimes against seniors and have found, again and again, that the victim was in high-risk circum-

stances—a secluded street, an isolated automatic teller machine, an off-hours service station, a high-crime district. One study of street robberies in an eastern city found that almost all the victims were both alone and in an isolated situation. Any isolated spot away from public view encourages criminality, while the mere presence of others deters most crimes. Also, certain districts of any city will be crawling with crooks, while other districts remain relatively crime-free. The overwhelming majority of crimes happen only in certain locations, at certain times, and under certain circumstances. Avoiding these is half the battle in crime protection.

3. *Failing to look before you leap.* Impulsiveness can be a charming personal trait, but when it leads to opening your front door to unidentified strangers, returning carelessly to your car in the evening, making offhand investments, blindly following professional advice, or haphazardly choosing a retirement community, it can be deadly. Robbers, con artists, and other nefarious characters count on the fact that some people will be impulsive. Much crime avoidance rests on coolheaded "checking it out."

4. *Having a victim-prone lifestyle.* Frequent intoxication, a perennial chip on the shoulder, a sarcastic conversational style that provokes ill will—all can increase our vulnerability to crime. Engaging in illegal activities, such as gambling, visiting prostitutes, or working shady deals, puts you cheek to jowl with the criminal underworld. Why needlessly ask for or make trouble?

5. *Complacency.* This risk usually involves either a

"nothing ever happens here" or a "just this once" attitude. Seniors who are well settled in their living arrangements and have escaped previous victimization are especially prone to this. Yet the main reason "nothing ever happened before" is probably all the good-sense precautions normally taken. People often don't realize that it is their routine crime-avoidance habits that have kept them crime-free, and so they may let down their guard. Or they get upset or get in a rush and fail to follow their ordinary security habits. Complacency is one of the criminal's best, most reliable accomplices.

#5

How Crime-Protection Tactics Work

In a nutshell, here's how crime avoidance works. Three things must be present for a crime to happen: (1) Someone with a criminal intent, (2) an available target, and (3) an opportunity. The old English proverb, "Opportunity makes the thief," is absolutely true. All protection strategies work by either making the target unavailable or by denying the criminal any opportunity or by making the risks so high that the would-be culprit backs off. If you think about this, you can see why thwarting works and even make up tactics to fit your own situations.

When you avoid high-crime locales, for instance, you are not an available target for a high concentration of people with nasty intentions. If you carry little cash, you might still be a target, but you've greatly reduced a thief's opportunity to steal from you. If you don't take a purse when you go out, there's no target for a grab-and-run purse snatcher. If there are senior women with purses around, but they are with companions and are in plain sight of other people, the purse thief has some targets, but very increased risk. We can make ourselves and our property unavailable (no target) or inaccessible (no opportunity). Often we can't entirely do either of these, but we can drastically reduce our exposure. And we can often make the risk too high to be worth it for the culprit. Even a desperate mugger probably wouldn't assail a foursome walking together or an older woman being escorted to her car by a security guard.

It is instructive to look at the world through a criminal's eyes. Smart or dumb, right or wrong in his judgment calls, he tries to figure his odds. It is certain that many times during your life, criminals have looked over you, your home, your car, and other possessions with greed in their hearts. But they passed you by and struck elsewhere or just went home. Why? Because your precautionary actions were effective, even though you may never have seen the crook. Maybe the would-be culprit saw there were two of you. Or he saw that the bag boy was helping you to your car with the groceries. Or he saw a light and heard a radio playing in your home.

Whatever a would-be criminal has in mind, he is encouraged or discouraged by the situation—*the circumstances determine whether or not a crime will actually occur.* Often changing just one thing will change the situation into a protected one. A little protection goes a very long way.

❖ T w o ❖

Protecting
Your Home Life

Your home is supposed to be your refuge amidst a sometimes uncertain world. But how safe is it from crime? That depends almost entirely on you and your neighbors.

You don't have to crouch fearfully inside your dwelling. But you do need to take steps to see that you are not unwittingly inviting crime. This goes double for seniors who spend more time at home and who are also sometimes prey to mobility-reducing afflictions such as arthritis.

The entries in this chapter lay out hard-won tactics, from criminology researchers, crime-prevention workers, and criminals themselves, for making your home life more secure. By the time you finish reading through these tips, you will see that there really is good news about protecting your home life: *Most would-be home intruders can be rather easily foiled.*

#6

Finding a Safe Place to Live

For one reason or another, seniors often find themselves wrestling with the question of where to live. Some are comfortable (or stuck) where they're at; others want or need to move. If you plan to relocate, security from crime should be a main consideration, because where you live can be the most vital factor in your day-to-day level of safety (see entry #4). Even if you don't plan to move soon, this data is useful for the future.

The beautiful brochures, videos, and magazine articles aimed at seniors about retirement and resettlement opportunities are advertisements, not balanced sources of facts. A local chamber of commerce or real estate developer strives to entice more than inform. So never make a decision only on their say so. The two main failings of such come-on advertisements are that they don't give you enough of the good and bad facts to make the best decisions, and their offerings are usually more expensive than the deals you can find on your own. Such promotions can come very close to being scams. The various "places rated" books should also be approached with caution because their profiles may be based on features that are of no concern to you, such as the availability of golf, high-tech medicine, or highbrow cultural events. A smaller town might well give you what you want at half the price. If you are a vegetarian naturopath who prefers Louis L'Amour Western novels to symphonies, for instance, such ratings may mean very little. Places-rated books also fail to give you breakdowns of ratings for the various districts within cities, which is the data that's usually most vital to know. For instance, people don't move to Houston, they move to some neighborhood in Houston, and different neighborhoods within the same city can range from wonderful to nightmarish.

The fact that some locale is popular with seniors and retirement community developers is not necessarily a reliable guide either. Several popular retirement areas, such as Florida and southern California, actually have rather high crime rates.

Never buy into any location without personally going there and checking it out *independently*. Get away from the promoters and talk with some of the residents, shopkeepers, and local police about the quality of life and the crime situation. (Many promoters routinely strive to keep out-of-towners from doing this.) It's also an excellent idea to get hold of a local map and subscribe to the local newspaper for a month to get a better idea of what's really going on and where.

Because the crime rates vary so greatly from district to district, you can live securely in most large metropolitan areas if you choose your neighborhood with thorough care. The neighborhood doesn't have to be posh and expensive; there are usually many safe, stable districts filled mostly with working-class people and retirees, often of mixed ethnic backgrounds. But it is important to assure yourself that the neighborhood is not rapidly deteriorating. Many older neighborhoods are stable and charming, while some are rapidly going to the wolves. Casual conversations with a half-dozen locals can quickly tell you which is the case.

A visual inspection of the prospective area is actually one of your best yardsticks for assessing its crime-proneness. Are the houses and buildings kept up? Are the streets kept clean? How well a neighborhood is kept up by the residents is the best barometer of the quality of life prevailing around there.

The other excellent indicator to check into is how transient the local population is. According to criminologists, areas with many transients and strangers virtually always have higher crime rates than areas with low population turnover. This holds true whether prices are expensive or modest. Ask around. In a low-turnover neighborhood, locals will have some idea of who their neighbors are, and most will have been living there at least a couple of years.

Real estate prices and rentals are usually lower in unstable, high-crime areas, but they're a very bad bargain.

Where you settle has lots of implications crime-wise. For example, the Illinois state attorney general's office found that car insurance coverage cost eight times as much in the Chicago Loop area as in a small downstate town. And Ray Johnson, the professional criminal turned eminent crime expert, notes, "Most residential burglaries are committed by youngsters who live within six to twelve blocks of the house being robbed."

If you do move to a new location, it's a wise idea to do a fresh assessment of your routine security habits. Learn the lay of the land, the populated areas, the safe havens, the risky spots, where public phones are, and so on.

#7

Crimeproofing Your Home's Exterior and Grounds

It's a virtual certainty that at one time or another burglars have cruised by your place and checked it out as a possible target. Convicted burglars report that they wouldn't bother to try dwellings that seem to present much difficulty unless they thought they contained especially tempting prizes. As I've said before, criminals play the odds, too. And *appearances* are what matter most to them. What first impression does your dwelling give to a would-be criminal?

Home security begins with your dwelling's exterior and grounds. Take a few minutes to go outside and walk all around your dwelling to see how tempting and accessible it might be to crooks. Do this even if you live in a housing complex or upper-story apartment, keeping in mind that most would-be intruders are young and agile.

Pay special attention to the often neglected side and back areas. Don't forget the garage, parking area, or any sheds. Are there ladders or benches or trellises that could be helpful to a would-be culprit?

Landscaping, trees, and fences should be such that all sides of the dwelling, especially entryways, are clearly visible. Foliage should be cut back so it provides no hiding place and does not obscure neighbors' view of the property—fences and tall hedges often give concealment to would-be intruders. Trees should be trimmed so they provide no roadway to balconies or upper story windows.

Exterior lighting should be sufficient to prevent deep shadow zones. Floodlights are not necessary; sixty-watt bulbs will do the job. A backyard light with a photoelectric switch that turns on automatically at dusk costs less than twenty dollars.

You'll especially want a clear, unobstructed view of the entrances you use for leaving and returning home and for outside chores, such as carrying out the trash, so do any trimming or lighting to make it so. For some reason, a neat and trim lawn with paper scraps and trash picked up has also proven to be a crime deterrent.

Most burglars are sneaks who don't want to be seen or heard and they almost always stay away from dwellings if there are signs that anyone might be at home. One of the biggest giveaways that no one is home is a darkened house with a porch light on. So always create the impression that someone is home, even when no one is. Two of the easiest ways to do this are to (1) always leave a light on somewhere inside the house and (2) have a TV or radio turned on low, preferably to a talk show. For just a few dollars you can also get timers to turn on lights and appliances while you're absent. This impression is especially important for seniors who live alone because it helps create the illusion of people at home.

Burglars look for concealment from public view, for ease of entry, and for the unlikelihood of detection. The preceding pointers should discourage them.

#8

Door and Window Security

My grandmother used to say, "Close the door, you're letting in flies." Today I'd tell my grandchildren, "Lock your doors and windows, you're letting in crooks." In 40 percent of home break-ins the culprits just walk through an unlocked door or crawl through an open window.

Eminent criminologists Michael Gottfredson and Travis Hirschi pointed out in a recent *Washington Post* article: "Solid research studies show that most ordinary crimes can be prevented by the presence of even the most minor obstacles; locks on doors, keys taken out of ignitions, reduced late-night hours for convenience stores, and the like. The typical burglary or robbery takes little effort, little time, and little skill."

There are a few highly skilled professional burglars who can beat just about any home security setup. But unless you (1) have very expensive valuables and (2) widely advertise the fact, these pros are almost certain not to bother with you. They perpetrate less than 1 percent of all break-ins.

Having half-decent locks on all potential entrances and using them regularly is half the battle in being safe at home and securing your possessions. There's universal agreement among crime experts that deadbolt locks offer the best protection because they are very hard to pick or jimmy open. (Most burglars don't know how to pick locks.) Ideally, these locks should be combined with solid core doors and sturdy door jambs. Even without this hardware, a simple rubber doorstop inserted under the door bottom can make the door surprisingly more break-in resistant. The average burglar spends only one minute to break in and stays less than ten minutes in the house; he is highly exposed during this time and knows it. So *anything* that slows him (or occasionally her) down will increase the likelihood that he'll just move off. Even when no one's home, he has no idea when someone might return or if a neighbor has seen his activity and called the police.

Be sure to comparison shop for any security devices or equipment, such as deadbolts. Prices at a discount store, like Wal-Mart, may be half what they are at regular chain stores or stores specializing in security equipment. It's ironic that you can get ripped off by price gouging in the process of buying security items. Simple, less expensive items are often as good for most people's needs as complicated high-priced ones. For instance, a $40 solid wood door rather than a $200 steel reinforced one will probably do for your security.

Door chains are popular but actually of limited value, unless made of case-hardened steel and mounted in such a way that an intruder can't reach through and unlatch them. A simple sliding bolt works better as a second lock.

If you are handy enough to hang curtains or do minor car repairs, you'll find home security items easy to install. If, like the author, you are all thumbs, you probably have a friend or relative who is handy. If you live in a condo or apartment complex, a member of the maintenance or security staff will probably help you for a few dollars. Or ask your neighbors to recommend a reliable handyman. Some senior groups will help with the installation at little or no cost.

Burglars often try to force side and back entrances because these are far less exposed to public view. Ironically, these are also the entry points often least well protected. Sliding bolts or a sturdy bar that drops into a wall bracket can be effective in your less-used entrances, and they still allow you to get out easily in case of an emergency. If you have an attached garage, check the door and lock leading into the dwelling—they are notoriously flimsy. Also, the door leading up from the basement warrants a lock or bolt.

To increase your own personal security, make your bedroom a "safe room" by installing locks on its door. That way, if you hear an intruder, you can go there and be safe. A chair wedged under the doorknob plus a wedge under the door will make even a hollow core door virtually impenetrable. However, if you hear an intruder, it is better to leave the dwelling and go to a neighbor for help if you can.

Locks that come with sliding glass doors are usually inadequate. But if you lay a broom handle or other sturdy piece of wood, cut to size, along the bottom runner, sliding doors can't be opened. You can get an additional lock from discount hardware stores that prevents the glass from being lifted off the frame. Doors with large windows in them are a special problem because a crook can break the glass and reach through. One solution is to install bars or heavy metal mesh over the glass.

There are a couple of other hard-won pointers about doors. First, *lock them*, even when you're just stepping over to the neighbor's for a minute or doing a bit of yard work. Second, do not leave an extra key hidden outside your dwelling. Criminals have shown an uncanny ability to find these hidden keys. It's a much better idea to exchange spare keys with a trusted neighbor or carry an extra one on your person in a different pocket.

Windows need some attention, too. They should be closed and locked when not in use and upon retiring. Triple-track windows are a good deterrent since they can provide three barriers, but they are expensive to install. Ordinary screens, well mounted and locked, can sometimes be an effective barrier. The little "butterfly" locks that come with ordinary windows are quite flimsy. You can get a second set of inexpensive window locks to back them up. If windows are reachable from the outside grounds they should only be opened far enough for ventilation. You can prevent them from being forced further open by window stops. Even a block of wood nailed inside the upper track or a strong nail driven into the side of the upper sill will do.

For basement windows, consider installing the kind of bars that can easily be lifted only from the inside or use heavy metal mesh. You could also permanently seal those that are never opened, but be sure to leave an easy fire exit.

Over 80 percent of local police precincts now have a crime prevention unit that will come out and do a free home security inspection for you, spotting weak points and outlining remedial options. When calling them, be sure to use their business hours number, not the emergency line. In some places, police-sponsored home security programs for seniors have cut burglaries 50 percent or more.

It's good to have the kind of curtains or drapes where you can see out but others can't see in, for at least some of your dwelling. If part of your house can't be observed from outside, it's hard for would-be intruders to tell whether or not anyone is present. Their doubts work in your favor.

One could ask, "Is all this stuff really worth doing?" From a mountain of solid evidence, the answer is a resounding yes.

#9

How About a Dog?

The most ancient alarm system for protection of homes and property, used over at least half the world, is a dog. Dogs give criminals enough extra uncertainty and risk that they tend to just move on by. In fact, the second most frequent recommendation from convicted burglars and rapists for protecting yourself from others like them is: "Get a dog."

The crime experts I've checked with advise not getting an attack dog for residences, because they tend to be high strung and can too easily maul the wrong person. A friendly pooch from your local animal shelter will serve at least as well in providing an alarm and a deterrent to lurkers. A dog can be especially valuable protection for seniors living alone or who have some impairment of vision, hearing, or mobility.

Dogs are most effective if they can be given the run of the house. It's also best to keep them inside most of the time. If they are out in the yard they can be more easily evaded or dealt with. I've also been told that female dogs tend to be more protective of their territory. The little dogs that yap incessantly from inside the house can actually be the most troublesome for prowlers.

In our neighborhood, any stranger is met by at least three barking dogs and a chorus of little yappers as he or she walks through. It would be hard for anyone to get within ten feet of a house without this alarm being sounded. Even new mail carriers are cautious.

A dog can provide companionship as well as security. And research evidence shows that having a pet often increases the health and lifespan of seniors. For instance, researcher Erika Friedmann found that heart patients with pets in their homes have a higher survival rate.

What if you can't have a dog where you live, or you are a cat lover? Modern electronics provides the answer.

#10

Home Security Alarm Systems

What about all the electronic home security devices now coming onto the market? Are they worth a hoot for increasing your protection? Yes—but you must pick and choose. And dodge high-pressure sales hype.

No alarm system is a 100 percent guarantee of security. There is always someone who will be able to handle or bypass it. But many crooks are scared off by signs that a home is equipped with one. So if you purchase an alarm, be sure to display the alarm decals prominently on outside windows. Homes with any kind of alarm are less likely to be hit. As one burglar put it, "So many houses *don't* have alarms; why bother with the ones that do?"

Convicted burglars say they are leery of dwellings with any kind of alarm system, and some (but not all) report that they always steer clear of them. And the FBI has estimated that a residence equipped with a full alarm system hooked into a monitoring station or the police is fifteen times less likely to be hit. If an alarm does go off, most culprits report that they just quickly grab whatever they can and flee, which cuts the losses to the residents.

Prices of security alarm devices have dropped dramatically in recent years, while their reliability, effectiveness, and ease of installation have continued to improve.

The principle all of them operate on is quite simple. Some kind of sensor detects an attempted or actual intrusion which triggers an alarm response. The response might be a bell or siren, flashing of the house lights, an automatic call to a monitoring station or the police, or all of the above. The culprit, neighbors, you if you're home, and maybe outside authorities know a break-in has been detected. Most modern alarms are wireless, which means they can be easily installed in any type of dwelling, and they will not be disarmed by a power outage. They can also be triggered by a portable "panic button" which you can carry around with you or place on your night stand.

There are two types of sensors. Perimeter alarms go off when a magnetic contact is broken if someone opens a protected door or window. Internal space alarms get triggered if they sense the motion or body heat of anyone who intrudes into the space they are covering. They work like your remote TV tuner.

You can tie all kinds of additional features into a basic system. For instance, timers can turn lights and appliances on and off in complicated sequences and smoke detectors and a medical emergency feature can be added. But past a certain point, such elaborate gadgetry may be money down the drain. There's a lot to say for a simple, inexpensive system that is easy to operate and easy to explain to others. Get one that is Underwriter's Laboratory approved and learn well how to operate and maintain it. If you are gone regularly during the day, leasing a system that is monitored by an outside agency, such as Brinks, might be your best bet. The leasing and installation cost around $200, and the monthly monitoring fee is around $20. An alarm system may also entitle you to an insurance discount—ask.

#11

Screening Callers at Your Door

Who's at the door?" is a question we seniors need to take seriously these days. Most of those who show up are harmless, maybe even welcome. But some are not. So without being overanxious, you should take some care. *Never open your door before finding out who is there and what their business is.*

The first point about visitors at your door is one that a surprising number of people get caught on. You don't have to go along with visitors' requests just to be polite. You don't have to answer their questions, listen to their spiel, let them demonstrate their product, contribute to their charity, or let them use your phone—and in most cases it's wisest not to. Every veteran police officer has had to deal with cases where seniors have been burglarized, assaulted, or conned because of such unnecessary politeness. *Politely refuse.*

One of the best security investments anyone can make is an inexpensive front door peephole with a wide-angle viewing lens. Then you can always screen your callers. If strangers come to another entrance, ask them to come around to the front.

In addition to a deadbolt and peephole, a sturdy chain is useful, especially when combined with a doorstop. Perhaps it won't stop a lunatic, but it gives some additional protection when you answer the door. When you don't know the delivery person, you can receive letters and small packages without fully opening your door by having the caller hand them through. Even better, however, have callers leave the item on the step and watch until they leave.

If people you don't know come to your door and ask to use your phone, don't let them in. At most, offer only to make the call for them while they wait outside.

If a caller claims to be from some agency or utility company and you are even vaguely suspicious, ask the person to wait while you make a call to verify the claim. Get the number yourself because any number the caller supplies could be that of an accomplice or friend. You can also ask to see credentials, but don't let the person just quickly wave something in the air. Ask the caller to hand the credentials to you, and look at them closely. If the caller mutters in protest, let him—after all, it's your home, your belongings, and your life.

When you do let workers, meter readers, or even grand-children in, it's wise to put any small valuables lying around out of sight so you still have them after the people leave. No reason to tempt anyone.

If you live in an apartment complex, for everyone's security, don't buzz the door open for anyone you don't know.

#12

Telephone Security Tips

For many seniors the telephone is virtually their main link with the outside world. And the telephone is a blessing that we use to talk to friends and loved ones, to find things out, or to call for help. It also allows others to reach us. Most incoming calls are just friendly or just bothersome. But a few are from characters with their own unwholesome schemes, so it's prudent to employ some security tips from the phone companies and the National Office of Consumer Affairs.

The basic tip is this: Don't give out personal information over the phone unless you know exactly who you're dealing with or you yourself initiated the call—and never to an unknown person. Don't answer personal questions. Never give your credit card number, your bank account number, any details about where you work or live, medical data, and so on to phone solicitors or inquirers. You don't even have to give your name. Unless you know who you're talking to and why, there's no telling what use any personal information you give might be put to. If the caller presses you, just hang up.

If the call is a wrong number, don't give your own name and number. If they ask who or what number they've reached, just say: "You have a wrong number."

There are good security tips to use if you have an answering machine. Unless you need to for business reasons, don't give your name or number on the message. A widely recommended message is something like this: "Hello. If you leave your name and number, we'll get back to you." Never say "We're not home." Say "we" even if you're living alone. It might cause some gossip among your acquaintances, but it will be discouraging to anyone with unfriendly intentions. Even the *impression* that there might be two or more people is much safer than the suspicion that there is only one.

If you get an obscene or abusive phone call, just hang up. Virtually all such characters are harmless, but why risk it? If such calls are repeated, contact your police and the phone company, who will explain your options. With modern systems, it is now much easier for authorities to trace these kinds of calls. Don't blow a whistle in the caller's ear; you might only rouse the vindictiveness of an unstable person.

I strongly suggest that you place a list of emergency numbers next to each of your phones. Studies have shown that people from the age of five to a hundred often have difficulty remembering phone numbers during the stress of an emergency. Once, when I'd been bitten by a dog, I couldn't recall the cab number I'd used a hundred times or even "911" for the life of me. But my wife had them right there by the phone.

The thing to keep in mind is that when unknown persons call, you don't know what they might be up to. So experts recommend "defensive answering" (similar to defensive driving).

#13

Safeguarding Your Mail

For me and most other seniors, the mail is a personal, professional, and financial lifeline, so there's good reason to see to its security. There are stiff federal penalties for tampering with the mails, but some crooks still do it. So how can we thwart them?

First, always pick up your mail as quickly as possible after delivery—which removes the thief's opportunity.

If you live in a single dwelling, by far the best arrangement is a mail slot that drops the mail inside your house. This accomplishes two things. First, it secures your mail from casual theft. And second, no one can see from an overstuffed mailbox that you aren't home. These slots are inexpensive and rather easily installed by a handyman or mechanically inclined friend, if you need help.

If your mailbox is observable from outside, and you'll be gone even for a day or so, arrange to have a trusted neighbor empty the box so it doesn't signal "nobody home" to passersby. If you live in a complex, with all the mail boxes together, ask a neighbor or the manager to do the same. Security mail boxes with enough room for several weeks' mail and featuring tamper-proof locks are also now available.

It's best to put either no name or more than one name on the box. If you're living alone, you don't want to broadly advertise it. If you're a single woman don't just use your initials because crooks now know this trick. Just put a fictitious name alongside yours.

The American Association of Retired Persons (AARP) has also pointed out the danger in leaving outgoing mail in an outside box. The raised flag is a signal to thieves.

If you receive any regular social security or pension checks, it is extremely prudent to have them deposited directly into your bank account, which your bank can arrange. One out of every several hundred checks delivered to residences is lost or stolen, while only one in several hundred thousand directly deposited presents any problem. If a social security check doesn't arrive when expected, wait three business days, then call the Social Security Administration at (800)722-1213. Usually you can expect a replacement check within thirty days—or in emergency circumstances, in as little as seven days. Direct deposit also prevents the risk of being robbed while cashing the check or carrying the money.

If you get large volumes of mail because you are operating a home business, you might want to consider using a post office box. The mail is more secure in a postal station and customers or clients you don't really know won't have your home address.

#14

Don't Forget About Garage Security

Garages, sheds, and other outside buildings offer special opportunities to thieves. *Garage break-ins are more than twice as common as residential break-ins.* Yet crime prevention officers routinely discover that virtually everyone is far more careless about their garages than their dwellings. Unsecured garages can be helpmates to crooks by providing places to lurk and tools for breaking into the house. And finally, if your garage is attached to the house it can provide an easy entry into your dwelling.

If you add up the value of all the things you may have in your garage—lawn implements, tools, hoses and ladders, paint, trunks, perhaps sports and hobby equipment—the total is likely to be at least several hundred dollars. You'd never leave all this lying on your curb for anyone to pick up. Why leave them in an unsecured garage?

Garage break-ins are mostly done by amateurs such as underage kids with delinquent streaks. Luckily, these are the culprits who are most easily discouraged. Usually they're not (yet) serious criminals and their garage break-ins are "treasure hunts" and adventures.

For the ordinary detached garage, a padlock of case-hardened steel, used unfailingly, will suffice. If the garage has windows, place dowels or nails in the upper track so they can't be raised. If you never open the windows you might even nail them permanently shut. If you want an electric garage door opener, many newer models have an automatic lock function that is very adequate. If you've turned your garage into a workshop or hobby shop with expensive equipment, consider adding a simple internal space alarm.

If your garage is attached to the house, security steps become more imperative. Attached garages should be included in any alarm setup you install.

Suburban houses typically have very poor locks and flimsy doors between the attached garage and the house. On top of this, investigators have found that half the time people fail to lock them at all. So this can be a weak spot in household security. An effective measure is to have a deadbolt lock plus a simple sliding bolt on the door leading into the dwelling and always use them.

If you live in a multidwelling complex with communal garage parking, insist, together with the other occupants, that management maintain some adequate level of overall security. There should be good lighting and locking devices, and management and occupants need to cooperate in seeing that the complex is not swarming with unidentified strangers. It is an excellent tactic to have an active homeowners' or tenants' association that takes up security matters.

However good or bad the complex's security is, stay alert going to and from your dwelling and your vehicle. Don't be so preoccupied or complacent that you fail to notice anything suspicious in your immediate surroundings. Even if the complex has internal TV monitoring and security personnel on duty, continue to be your own guardian—remain alert.

#15

Dealing with Break-ins

In about one out of every eight burglaries, someone is home when a thief breaks in. In almost all these cases, the intruder didn't realize that someone was home.

There is one firm principle, strongly advised by both the police and convicted felons, to follow in case of a break-in. *Do not confront the intruders.* Even if you're armed to the teeth, don't accost them or block their exit in any way. Many culprits in prison for residential assault said they had never intended to attack anyone, but only defended themselves because they were confronted and cornered by an occupant.

Burglars usually have no more desire to run into you than you have to run into them. The intruder is nervous, in a hurry, and facing an unknown setup. Chances are good that he is under the influence of drugs or alcohol. Chances are about fifty-fifty that he is armed and, even if not, he may be carrying tools that can quickly become assault weapons. Chances are also good that you'd be facing more than one culprit. The apprehending of offenders is strictly police business. If you try to confront them, the situation, at the very least, could turn into one of armed robbery. As studies have shown, even if you "win" a scuffle or a shootout, you stand a strong chance of being injured in the process.

So what do you do?

If you hear an intruder or your alarm goes off, leave the house immediately if you can. Go to a nearby neighbor or public phone and call the police. The next best move is to go to your safe room, lock and barricade the door, then phone the police. Then make lots of noise so the culprits will know someone is home and active. They will almost certainly grab what they can and flee at this point, so take no action that will block their exit. Some crime experts recommend yelling something like: "Take what you want and leave; the police are on their way!" If you are armed you might say so loudly. From the intruders' viewpoint, this has become a "crazy" situation that they'll want to get out of as fast as they can. Some habitual burglars cut phone lines, but most amateurs don't. If your phone isn't working, get to your safe-room window and start yelling. If you have an alarm system that hasn't been tripped by the forced entry, push your "panic button" and activate it. If you have a personal shriek alarm or whistle, blow it. If you can reach a radio, TV set, or record player, turn it up to ear-shattering, neighborhood-rousing volume.

If you awaken to find a prowler in your room, pretend to remain asleep until they finish their foraging and leave. The odds are they won't bother you physically.

When you arrive home from being out and there are any signs that there may have been a break-in, do not enter. Go immediately back to your car or to a neighbor and call the police. Have them check the premises out.

#16

Defending Your Home and Possessions

As seniors, we tend to feel strongly that our home is our castle, and we want to hold on to what we've got. But how far should we go in defending our things? And what kinds of defenses are effective?

The topic of defending your property and yourself while at home is strewn with moral and practical questions. It is also strewn with misleading advertisements by very profitable industries that are playing on fears of crime. So we need to pick our way through this subject carefully.

We've seen that the last thing most intruders want is any confrontation with occupants. Would-be intruders can never be sure what a particular occupant is capable of. One study of burglars found that what they feared most was not arrest and conviction, but being blown away by some resident. So just being visibly at home is an effective deterrent to most culprits.

There are three levels of self-defense: (1) unarmed, (2) nonlethal weapons and devices, and (3) lethal weapons. Each type has its usefulness, but each has severe limitations that promoters too often gloss over. And law officers complain that each can give people a false sense of security so that they neglect more basic and reliable crime avoidance measures.

Unarmed defense involves physically resisting intruders with your own body—fists, fingernails, feet, elbows. If intruders come upon you in your home, the two most common outcomes will be that they will flee or that the situation will turn into simple robbery. Almost all experienced crime experts recommend that you not physically attack or resist perpetrators unless your life or the life of another is threatened. This is especially true if they are armed with guns or knives or there are more than one of them. Physical resistance greatly increases the chance of injury, and even if you "win" you may be severely injured in the process. Also, don't lecture or berate the robbers—such actions will only risk angering them.

So do all those widely promoted self-defense classes—rape defense, karate, aikido—have any value? Yes, but in subtle ways, and with limitations. Aside from anything else, these regimens are good exercise and health tonics and people sometimes find enriching truths in their philosophies. They also have a direct crime-protection boost. Evidence shows that the students' increased self-assurance somehow telegraphs to would-be offenders. Women graduates even report a steep drop in verbal harassments. There is no age limit on learning most of these techniques.

But even highly skilled self-defense instructors say they wouldn't take on someone with a gun because they know they're not quicker than a bullet. Nor would they resist someone with a knife unless directly attacked. They also say that if there is more than one assailant this greatly complicates any physical resistance. So these techniques are far from a crime protection cure-all in spite of what the course promoters and action movies would have us believe.

Nonlethal weapons can be just about anything—a rolling pin, walking stick, pair of scissors, hammer, or tire chain. Commercial products, such as Mace, are currently being heavily promoted. But the claims for the effectiveness of such products are very questionable. People who have them often think they're better protected than they actually are, so they become careless about other security measures. The question is, "Will the use of a nonlethal weapon just enrage an assailant instead of intimidating or incapacitating him?" The answer is, "Maybe, maybe not." Whether to resist with nonlethal weapons is a decision that can be made only by the individual on the spot. If at all possible, avoiding confrontation and using escape tactics are far more preferable.

Now we come to lethal weapons—guns. The U.S. Constitution gives us the right to bear arms, and half of all American households now possess some sort of firearm. But how effective are they in crime protection?

Some twenty thousand criminals are killed or wounded annually by guns in the hands of private citizens and a great many more are brought to justice or scared off. Older men and women who have gotten sick and tired of the crime menace are buying guns and learning to use them in increasing numbers. And there's no question that guns have sometimes been effective protection in citizen-criminal confrontations.

Now for the downside. A gun is not worth a hill of beans if (1) you can't get to it, (2) you're not trained in its use, or (3) intruders break in while you're away. Firearms will do no good protecting your home when you are absent; instead they will be a thief's prize. And again, guns can sometimes give residents a false sense of security so that they are careless about maintaining more basic protective measures.

If a firearm is unloaded and locked away, it may be of no use in an emergency. Yet, if it is loaded and handy by your bedside, it becomes an ever-present threat for grandchildren and other visitors. In fact, a recent study by the U.S. Conference of Mayors concluded that guns were more dangerous to families than to criminals.

Guns are dangerous to everyone around if the owner has not been trained to be competent in their maintenance and use. One needs to know about their cleaning and storage, different types of ammunition, safety procedures, and how to shoot them. For instance, it takes real practice to hit something with a handgun.

If you want a gun, there are lots of choices. Unless you are a gun hobbyist, there's no reason to get an expensive or elaborate firearm. A small caliber revolver, .22 caliber rifle, or twenty-gauge shotgun are all easy to care for, lightweight, and easy to use. Comparison shop, and don't be misled into buying expensive, complicated wares.

You should know that firearms are one of the items most prized by thieves, so you'll need to secure them while you're away from home.

Since the last thing most burglars want is any confrontation with an occupant, taking measures to see that your dwelling always appears secure and occupied is still the most reliable tactic of all.

#17

Protecting Your Money and Valuables

We enjoy having money and valuables—and so do thieves. They operate from the profit motive, just like the rest of us. An interesting finding, from anonymous self-report studies, is that most people admit having swiped money and small valuables from older people in their own families when they were kids.

The world is a wonderland of potential riches in the mind of a thief. Burglars and robbers presume, rightly, that most senior residents who've attained even modest success in life will have some valuable items in their homes. Walk through your dwelling's interior and look around, thinking like a burglar. What could you grab or easily find and take away in ten minutes? What do you see that a thief might like to have or be able to sell to a fence for 10 percent of its face value? Your inspection might leave you feeling wide open and vulnerable, but there are some remedial steps that you can take.

Don't have any more cash lying around than you can afford to lose. A good idea is to have only a modest cash reserve, say fifty to a hundred dollars, hidden away somewhere in your dwelling. And be very creative in where you hide it. Here are some ideas other people have successfully used: in old garden gloves hanging in the basement, inside the pages of a worn reference book, taped behind the last page of a wall calendar, buried inside a box of Christmas tree ornaments, in a pocket sewn inside the sleeve of an old housedress or the leg of an old pair of work pants. Use your creative imagination.

Time is of the essence to a criminal. He will look through the most likely hiding places and almost never take the time to search thoroughly places that are hard to reach or take much time and effort to pull apart. Most burglars are opportunistic, not skillful; they will usually only steal what is readily available. Most burglaries have a duration of under fifteen minutes.

The first place thieves usually head for is the master bedroom because they know that four times out of five they can easily find valuable jewelry, expensive watches, and spare cash there. Most people put valuables in similar places, so burglars follow similar routines when robbing a house. The second round of their search is through the living room, dining room, and family room. Here they check for silverware, expensive collections, and electronic items that are easily portable, such as VCRs, stereos, and small TVs. A thief will almost never even go into a basement.

If you have a gun by your bedside at night, it needs to be hidden away each day.

There are places *not* to hide cash or small valuables. Anywhere in the master bedroom is iffy; don't put them under mattresses, under the bed, in medicine cabinets, the refrigerator or freezer. Most crooks also know about the phony electrical outlets and safes that look like vegetable cans that are so widely advertised.

If you decide on a home safe, it should never be the portable kind—thieves just carry them off and open them at their leisure. Any home safe should be both permanently floor mounted in concrete and concealed. Since very few burglars are pros, this will ordinarily be adequate security—especially if an alarm is sounding.

Some seniors have successfully thwarted burglars by secreting their cash and really valuable jewelry somewhere besides the bedroom, then leaving a few dollars and some look-alike costume jewelry lying around. (Most people, including thieves, can't tell the difference between expensive jewelry and well-crafted costume items.) If an intrusion does happen, your aim is to cut your losses and make a successful "score" more difficult for the thief.

Larger valuables, such as TVs, VCRs, computers, or antiques, usually can't be hidden. There are three approaches for protecting larger valuables, none of which is entirely satisfactory.

The first is tie-down locks. These "bolt" the item to a heavy anchoring fixture, such as a wall, door frame, or radiator. Tie-down locks consist of two strongly adhesive plates, one attached to the item, one attached to the anchor, with a case-hardened steel chain and padlock connecting the two plates. The chain is extremely resistant to saws or cable cutters and it is virtually impossible to pry the plates loose. With your key you can unlock the valuable and move it, but you'll need a new adhesive plate to secure it again in a new location. You can buy these tie-downs in many discount chain stores.

The second thing you can do about large valuables is to etch your social security number or driver's license number and state's initials on their surfaces as part of the national

Operation ID Program. Your local police precinct or library will lend you the electric tool for doing so free of charge. They will also supply the decals to put on your windows that warn that you are an Operation ID participant.

Operation ID is not a cure-all for the crime problem but it does help accomplish several things:

1. Theft is discouraged, because fences are less willing to take items so marked.

2. Officials can identify stolen items in the possession of suspected burglars. The etched IDs provide superb evidence for prosecuting crooks.

3. Officials can sometimes trace the movement of such items from thief to fence and onward, which aids in the breakup of criminal rings.

4. Recovered items can be traced and returned to their owner. The chances of recovering items so marked is not great, but sometimes you get lucky. And if you have strong suspicions about who did the stealing, the police can investigate and proceed accordingly.

The third thing you can do is get adequate insurance coverage. Because of deductibles and the hassles involved with replacement, you never come out even if you are burglarized. And some items may be irreplaceable. But with insurance your financial loss is reduced to a more bearable level.

Most insurance companies will provide you with a handy booklet in which to record your household items and their serial numbers. This might seem like going to a lot of trouble, but studies have shown that people almost inevitably underestimate how many belongings they have, and their value, if they don't make an itemized record. This inventory should be kept with your other permanent records. If you aren't up to this paperwork, at least take pictures or make a videotape of your most valuable large items for authentication purposes if you ever have to file an insurance claim.

If you are renting, buy a renter's insurance policy to cover your personal belongings. They run about $150 per year to insure $20,000 worth of possessions in most areas. (Your landlord's policy doesn't cover your own personal property.)

In getting insurance, again, the watchword is comparison shop to avoid the crime of overpaying. For instance, you should call three different well-established companies. Also ask about discounts they offer, for seniors, for nonsmokers, for dwellings with crime-protection measures. Get replacement coverage, not a cash-value policy. It costs maybe 15 percent more but is worth it. Otherwise the depreciation over time of your valuables will drastically reduce the size of any settlement. If you have a valuable collection or expensive computer setup you should also check into an additional "floater" policy to cover these.

A word to the wise—the main reason burglary losses are often so devastating is that the victim never got around to applying the preceding tactics.

#18

Household Activities
Precautions

Seniors spend time around the home, doing many activities, such as cooking, laundry, showers, hobbies, entertaining visitors, and so on. Most of us also do outside yard work, sit on the porch, barbecue, have garage sales, and the like just outside our dwellings. Here are a few pointers, crime-wise, to keep in mind while doing all these things.

When you are preoccupied with doing something in one part of your home, the other parts are unoccupied. And when you are out in the yard, the whole dwelling is unoccupied. These obvious facts are too often overlooked and can result in a needless crime. The main culprits are grab-and-run amateur thieves, but one can also be vulnerable to more serious crimes.

When you go from one area of your home to another, always take a moment to see that things are secure. If you have a door open for ventilation, close and lock it before going off to the bathroom or to make a couple of phone calls. If you go down to the basement to do laundry, or upstairs to take a bath or nap, be sure the main-floor entrances and windows are closed and locked. Many people have lost purses, cameras, or heirlooms by not doing this.

When you're doing something around the outside of your home, you have a couple of security choices. You can lock everything up and carry the key with you. Or you can lock up everything but the entrance nearest you, so that you can quickly get back inside in case of trouble. If you sit on your front porch in the evening, for instance, you could leave your front door unlocked but be sure back and side doors are secured.

Entertaining visitors usually involves lots of bustling activity. And it will usually happen that guests will be in parts of your home while you are busy somewhere else. Now we must face the fact that a surprising percentage of people have a touch of larceny in their hearts. And most people are a bit curious—nosy. So take these truths under advisement. I confess, for instance, that when I was an urchin I often swiped change and candy from the purses of my grandmother and our guests. Most of the people I've talked to did the same thing. Your personal letters or diary may also draw inquisitive eyes.

Picnic or barbecue yard gatherings are especially likely to create situations where your dwelling is wide open to friend and foe alike because of all the running in and out. It's wise to put away cash, small valuables, and intimate personal items before such get-togethers.

Extra precautions are also required if you or your landlord are in the process of selling your dwelling. This means that a fair number of strangers may be traipsing through your premises, and they are often not very well screened by the real estate people. Also, real estate people often ask that residents not be present when they show the property, but I'd advise against this as long as your belongings are there. It's good to firmly curtail any unannounced showings and to check through the house and secure valuables before the prospects arrive.

If you hold garage sales, they deserve some precautions, too. They usually involve a flurry of activity, so arrange to have a friend or neighbor with you. (Consider a joint sale.) This will cut down on petty theft and help maintain security. If you can't get anybody to help, consider postponing the sale until you can.

Take extra care to see that your dwelling is secured during the sale. And don't let strangers into the house to use the phone or bathroom. Also, put away excess cash as it accumulates. Don't needlessly give out personal information during the sale, either. Some culprits cruise garage sales as an opportunity to scout out dwellings and neighborhoods.

Post firm hours—say, early morning to 1:00 P.M.—and stick to them. Don't show leftover stuff to late callers if you don't know them. Double-check that everything is secure again when the sale is over.

Perhaps the basic point about activities around the home is this: Don't become complacent because you are on your own turf and "nothing ever happens." Maintaining routine security will help see that nothing ever does.

#19

Living Alone Securely

The U.S. Census Bureau tells us that over a third of our senior population now lives alone—by either choice or necessity. Living alone has its benefits, such as freedom to do whatever you want. Seniors often prefer it because they can maintain their own independence. (One interesting result of this trend is the fast-growing "singles world" of those over sixty.)

The evidence suggests that those who live alone are not any more crime-prone, but there are some special risks. First, your dwelling may be unoccupied a greater share of the time if you work, do volunteer activities, or go out frequently. The more often you are away from home, the more important burglary prevention measures become. Second, with only one person around, there's a lower activity level, which may be apparent to outsiders unless remedial steps are taken. Third, because of the false myths discussed earlier, crooks may think that older people living alone are easy pickings.

If you have just started living alone due to recent widowhood or a suddenly empty nest, realize that your security is now up to you in ways it might not have been before. The people you had been living with may have been creating a security umbrella that you took for granted. The remedial steps are easy and you can do them, but crime protection is now in your own hands.

If possible, when shopping, socializing, and so on, vary your daily routines so no outsider can easily predict when you will and won't be home.

Don't widely volunteer the fact that you're living alone. Crooks pick up data from tradespeople, meter readers, workers, even mail carriers. In fact, feel free to lie that you have a housemate to anyone you don't know well. Most honest people don't realize that many crooks develop and use wide information nets. The old saying, "The walls have ears," is far too true.

All the regular security tips apply when you live alone, but those for making your dwelling seem occupied are doubly important. Get an automatic timer from a local discount store to turn your radio or another noise-making appliance on when you're out. Have an inside light on at night and vary which light you turn on. This leaves a casual observer in doubt, which is exactly what you want. Have a lock on your bedroom door and a battery- or aerosol-operated personal alarm.

Some seniors have gotten together with trusted neighbors and purchased wireless two-way radios so they can come to each other's rescue in case of trouble. These devices have a range of around three blocks and are battery operated, so they can't be silenced.

Millions of people live alone safely and you can too, by making a few prudent provisions.

#20

Build a Network of Allies

Seniors, faced with the menace of crime, are rediscovering the fact that there's strength in numbers. Joining together with neighbors is the oldest, and still one of the most effective, forms of defense against crime. Many members of the animal kingdom do it, and next to personal protection measures, it's the most effective step you can take. In studies of convicted burglars, the majority said that merely being noticed by a neighbor was enough to thwart them. Most said they'd just leave if noticed by an area resident, and leave for sure if anyone challenged them by asking who they were or what they were doing. When almost everyone knows who their neighbors are, crime rates drop.

There are two excellent reasons to turn all your neighbors into nodding acquaintances: (1) people are much more likely to help nodding acquaintances than strangers, and (2) everyone can more easily spot who doesn't belong.

Home security measures backed up by a network of neighborhood or tenant mutual aid and support provides a double layer of protection from almost every kind of crime. Studies amply demonstrate that Neighborhood Watch and similar programs work, sometimes cutting crime rates in half or more—and sometimes even taking back overrun neighborhoods from the criminals. It's also nice to have not just your dwelling but also the streets around where you live be safe.

Starting a network of allies need involve no more than talking with a couple of your close-by neighbors and agreeing to watch out for each other a bit. There are a couple of interesting things about doing this. One is that people who have little or nothing else in common will forge security alliances. The other is that people are usually willing to help others they are even slightly acquainted with, while they often remain indifferent and unwilling to get involved for total strangers. You don't need to become boon companions—just allies in crime protection.

There's a bit more to building a durable, successful neighborhood crime protection network than "Hi, neighbor," although *any* mutual action is a worthwhile step. The more local residents who get involved, the better, for one thing. Even in high-crime locales, most citizens are law-abiding and desirous of security. When a few residents become interested, the next step is to contact the crime-prevention unit of your local police department and arrange a working liaison with them. The police have come to love neighborhood crime protection networks because they've discovered that it helps them do their own job. Whatever your neighborhood's level of security organization, make the police into major allies and partners in crime prevention. (See entry #21.)

By itself, a Neighborhood Watch–type program won't necessarily stop the burglar who coolly chooses his target dwelling because it looks unsecured and unoccupied. So it's necessary to continue your personal security routines. What such programs do is make the whole neighborhood riskier and more discouraging to malefactors—so they are likely to go elsewhere. Post signs (supplied by local police) that your area is protected by Neighborhood Watch.

Crime protection works best on a collective, cooperative basis. And a person's network of allies can stretch out far beyond the immediate neighborhood to include coworkers, old friends, people in local senior organizations and agencies—on and on. You already probably have something of a network; a bit of effort can expand it greatly into a virtual mutual-aid society.

Such a network has lots of other benefits; it can be a source of information and referrals, help in times of trouble, and a means of collective action, support, and companionship. For instance, about three out of five people find jobs through their support network. An even more interesting research finding is that seniors in a support network are less likely to see a doctor, less likely to get sick, handle stress better, and have higher levels of antibodies that protect against disease.

Even if you live quietly and see few people, making a few contacts with those around you can quickly produce a web of allies. The mere presence of others will halt most crimes in progress. And we really do greatly outnumber the bad guys.

#21

Partnership with the Police

We often expect too much from our police and government regulatory agents. By themselves they cannot keep us out of crime's way. In many cases, authorities can only respond to crimes already committed—which isn't much help to the victims. So our immediate personal security is a do-it-yourself job. Yet the police are a vital and necessary component in our overall protection program.

Besides our neighbors, law enforcement agents remain our best, most steadfast friends in crime prevention. It has been fashionable in some circles to bash the police lately, but think for a moment—where would we be without them? That cop who maybe hassled you about your speeding would be the most welcome sight in the world if you were being bothered by rowdies or heard a prowler. Police have an outstanding record of aiding seniors. Enforcement officers help thousands of older people every day and save countless lives every year.

Aside from responding to emergencies and working to keep the peace, the police provide the necessary partnership to make block and neighborhood security programs truly effective. Because most actual crime situations are local, your local police (and agency personnel) are usually far more important to your daily safety than any distant politicians.

Police are the repository of data about crimes, suspects, and suspicious situations. The importance of "telling the police" just can't be overstressed. Careful studies by the U.S. Justice Department have uncovered the fact that less than half the crimes against persons and only one-fourth of property crimes are ever reported to the authorities. Reasons for not reporting range from embarrassment and shame to fear of reprisal to "why bother" apathy. This gross underreporting only makes life safer for the *criminals*. An estimated 95 percent of the data officers have to work with comes from private citizens.

There are two vital reasons for reporting crimes and suspected crimes, even anonymously, to the police. First, although the likelihood of a crook being convicted for committing any single crime is shockingly low, their chance of eventually being nailed is almost certain.

Second, it is very important to nip crime in the bud in a neighborhood before it takes root and begins to spread like crabgrass. An active police-neighborhood partnership has proven the most effective way to do this. (You can report crimes and suspicions anonymously on the national toll-free hotline We Tip, 1-800-78-CRIME.)

It takes persistence over time for the police to break up lawlessness, so don't expect immediate results after supplying them with information. In most cases they have to abide by rules of evidence and other constraints, so be patient and remain cooperative if you can. You need them and they need you.

Coming and Going Crime-free

We seniors venture outside the security of our homes because we want to and we must. And the news media keep telling us stories about how dangerous such trips can be. Comings and goings out into the world can be dangerous. Yet they needn't be. After all, millions of older people come and go safely every day. Sometimes we are just lucky, but mostly we do so by taking some simple precautions.

The entries in this chapter outline security procedures to use under a wide variety of circumstances when going out. Some of these tactics have almost become time-worn clichés. But they are so widely advised for a very good reason—*they work.*

#22

Going Out Safely:
Some Vital Basics

The United Nations Universal Declaration of Human Rights asserts, "Everyone has the right to life, liberty, and security of person." What is so insidious about criminals is that they menace these basic human rights. Yet we don't have to become prisoners inside our own homes. For seniors, the basic trick to going out safely is to take steps so that we are not lone, isolated, reachable targets.

For starters, *develop the inflexible habit of doing a final check before going out* to see that entrances are closed and locked, that there's a light on and a radio playing, and that the house alarm, if you have one, is activated. Don't leave without doing this, any more than you'd leave home without putting on your clothes.

If at all possible, go out with a companion. When the San Jose Police Department conducted an undercover investigation of crimes against seniors, one major finding emerged. Criminals almost always left older people alone if there were more than one, even when one of the older persons appeared frail. Two people are always more than twice as safe as one. Other findings were that criminals look for seniors who walk in isolated areas, who carry easily snatched purses, who are coming out of banks on the first and fifteenth of the month, and who follow inflexible and predictable routines.

Many times it isn't feasible to have someone else along. The next best thing is to carry out your activities in such a way that other people are always around you. Avoid isolated places and circumstances, such as secluded sections of parking lots or dark side streets. If you can go with a companion *and* stay around populated places you will be doubly secure.

Strive to always remain in public view. If you are out alone and notice anything suspicious or threatening, your best immediate strategy is to get to where other people are—the more public the better. Isolated places are dangerous to honest citizens, and public places are dangerous to would-be culprits.

Always try to leave enough time so that you are not rushed. People in a rush are much more likely to scrimp on the effective security measures they ordinarily take. Seniors in a hurry have been known to leave their front door wide open, leave their keys in the ignition, even run headlong into the arms of a mugger by not watching where they were going—things they otherwise would never do.

When possible, vary your routines, so no one can precisely predict when or where you'll be coming and going or when you'll be gone for certain. If you can't vary your schedule much because of work or other commitments, you can refrain from telling many people about it.

Your highest-risk times are traveling to your destination and traveling back home again. This is when robberies, assaults, rapes, purse snatchings, and other unpleasantries are most likely to happen, so stay alert to your immediate surroundings during these transits. The entries that follow give pointers on specific risk circumstances, but the general point is to make yourself less vulnerable when you come and go by staying tuned in to what's going on around you.

When you carry less cash and fewer valuables, you have less to lose. It's also good to carry a bit of cash and change for the phone in a separate pocket, perhaps sewn inside your clothing. Carry only the credit cards you will be using. Also, be careful about showing much cash when paying for purchases—criminals are keen observers and large bills tempt them. Reach into your wallet or purse and take out only the bills you need. Don't use an automatic teller machine in a risky area, at night, or if you are alone and isolated. Getting a check-cashing card from grocery stores is much safer. Also, consider where you're going in choosing what jewelry and watches to wear. Dress in such a way that you don't stand out as an especially attractive target.

You can safely go out at night if you take a few precautions. Three or four people provide even more security when you go out on the town. The earlier evening hours are also safer than late at night when what the police refer to as the "night-crawlers" come out. Besides, "early bird" suppers and movies are much cheaper. It's best to go only to locales you're familiar with at night and leave exploring new places for the daylight hours.

Stay together. One lone person should not drop off or retrieve the car. The managements of the places you go to are usually keenly interested in avoiding any incidents because of the bad publicity and possible legal consequences. So they'll probably be eager to help you if you run into problems or threats. And don't go off alone even briefly if you've had a few drinks. Persons who show signs of intoxication are especially inviting to criminals.

Finally, don't be needlessly provoking or contentious while conversing with others, because you might provoke a violent response. With some of the unstable and drug-hazed people running around these days, it's just not worth the risk.

You could possibly ignore every one of the foregoing tips time and time again with nothing ever happening to you. Yet the odds would start running against you. On the other hand, following these strategies consistently you might go where you want, and do what you want, and remain out of crime's way all of your life.

#23

Safe Walking and Jogging

Government studies show that in 1960 only one-fourth of our adult population exercised regularly; now two-thirds do. And this includes an ever-increasing number of seniors. (Exercise often does more for your good health than a doctor can.) Walking and jogging regularly are two favorites among older people, and a few security steps can virtually ensure safety while doing so.

Know the territory you walk or jog in. It's wise to know where populated rest stops, phones, and public establishments are, as well as the secluded, isolated places and rowdy hangouts to avoid. Especially in the evening or the quiet very early morning hours, stay in familiar territory. Explore new routes only at the times when there are lots of other people around. Here's an odd fact about people that's even true of animals: On familiar turf they display more self-assurance and self-assertiveness. Somehow this telegraphs to would-be offenders so that the person is less vulnerable.

Walking or jogging with a friend or your dog is an excellent idea. And whether alone or with someone, it's wise to stay out of isolated areas and off secluded paths. If you study newspaper crime stories you find again and again that seniors who got into trouble while exercising were alone and in some isolated place. Unpopulated areas, such as wilderness trails, secluded parks, and nonresidential streets, are risky because there are no fellow citizens around and the bad guys know it. Also, stay clear of heavy growths of foliage, parked vans, stretches of abandoned buildings, and the like, which could provide concealment for an assailant. Such places were a lot safer when we were growing up than they are today.

Don't walk or run with a Walkman headset on because it reduces your awareness of your immediate surroundings. On residential streets walk or jog against the traffic; that way you are far less accessible to anyone in a vehicle.

Don't be an inviting target for robbers by wearing expensive rings, jewelry, or watches. Old sweat clothes are ideal; then even if would-be culprits are lurking somewhere along the way, they'll pass you up. Because you are exercising, there's really no reason to carry much money anyway, beyond a small amount for the phone or refreshments.

If you walk a lot, consider getting a cane or walking stick, even one you make from a sturdy branch. This discourages troublemakers. And it also is useful in dealing with loose dogs. Because of crime fears, a growing number of residents now have suspicious and unfriendly dogs that sometimes get out. Such dogs have been a problem in the last three neighborhoods our family has lived in. If you are assailed by a dog, report it to the police immediately. Owners are liable for what their dogs do and you'll help save someone else from getting mauled.

Older people may be prone to such medical mishaps as heart attacks or strokes, which is another main reason to stay near other people and in your own familiar territory when exercising.

If you are mugged while out exercising, immediately surrender your valuables without a fuss and get away. (See entry #29, "Dealing with Muggings and Holdups.")

The latest research suggests that a half hour of running or walking three times a week can cut a senior's chances of dying from a heart attack or cancer in half, and it can improve the quality of life even for those in their nineties. And a few precautions will make it safer.

#24

Vehicle Security
for Seniors

There are a number of crime protection issues involving motor vehicles. We need to move to and from them safely, be secure while driving, and protect our possessions and the cars themselves from theft. Even if you yourself don't drive, the following car security basics are worth knowing when you ride with others.

Complacency is perhaps the biggest crime risk factor involving vehicles, because complacency leads to carelessness. When people believe "nothing ever happens," they don't lock up when running into a convenience store for milk or when parking in a friend's supposedly safe neighborhood, or they leave packages on the passenger seat in a crowded mall parking lot, or they get preoccupied planning supper while walking back to their car. Such complacency can become a criminal's best friend.

Wherever you go, while driving and when you get out, always lock all vehicle doors. Close all windows tight, and take the keys with you when you leave the car. (In one-fifth of all car thefts the keys are left in the ignition.) Be sure your door, the passenger door, and the back doors are all locked, both while driving and when you leave the car. Roll the windows down no more than an inch or two for ventilation or to speak with someone. It's important to secure your vehicle even while driving to prevent unwelcome intrusions when you're going slow or stopping for signals. With all doors and windows secured, your vehicle can serve as a pretty effective sanctuary. These precautions also greatly reduce the risk of being "carjacked."

Park as close as you can to where you're going. Avoid the isolated sections of parking lots and areas where lighting is poor. In the evening, don't park on side streets to save a parking fee. Always take a moment to glance around the immediate area you're about to park in. If you notice anything suspicious or even questionable, pull out and park somewhere else.

If you have any physical disability, a reduced-mobility condition such as severe arthritis, or a chronic health problem, check with your doctor about getting a "handicapped person" sticker. You can then park in handicapped zones, which are close to entrances, and increase your safety.

Highway patrols and auto clubs have developed recommendations for staying crime-free while driving. Maintaining your vehicle in good working order usually heads their lists— tune ups, adequate tires, brakes in order, and so on. The California Highway Patrol advises making a habit of never falling below a quarter tank of gas—extra gas in the tank is like a bit of extra money in the bank.

Try always to put a safe distance between yourself and any erratic motorists. They may be stoned out of their senses or mad at the world, but you don't want to find out. If they yell insults at you, grit your teeth and let it go. At most, get their license number and report them to the authorities. If somebody starts playing road games with you, take the next safe exit and get to a gas station or other public place. If they follow you, do not drive to your home; drive to a populated location or the police station and report the matter.

If you do a lot of driving alone, consider getting a CB radio or cellular phone. That way you can quickly contact emergency services and the authorities. But don't open your car window to anyone except recognizable authorities or repair workers. Joining the American Automobile Association (AAA) is also an excellent investment because of its emergency and other services.

Even when you keep your car in good working order, mechanical breakdowns occasionally occur. If this happens, follow the tactics outlined in entry #27, "What to Do If You Get Stranded."

Whenever you need to stop temporarily, find a well-lighted, well-populated place, if possible. If you are alone and have a flat tire or other car trouble, drive slowly along the shoulder until you reach a gas station or service store. Even if the tire gets shredded, you'll reach a place of greater safety this way. This is especially wise at night and for women.

One word covers the subject of picking up hitchhikers. Don't.

When returning to your vehicle, always take a moment to scan the immediate area and see that nothing is out of the ordinary. Do this as an inflexible habit even if it's daytime and a busy parking lot. If you sense anything suspicious, turn around, go back where you came from, and get help. Most grocery and department stores have employees who will help you to your car and most professional buildings and malls have security personnel who will escort you and see you safely away. Don't hesitate to use these services. And don't neglect your intuitive feelings that something is amiss. Nobody really knows where intuitions come from, but through the centuries survivors have always relied on them.

As you approach your car, look to see that it hasn't been broken into and glance underneath the car, which is where robbers are now sometimes hiding. Also, look to see that no one is hiding inside before you get in.

When you drive someone to where they are going, stay put long enough to see that they get inside safely. And ask anyone who gives you a lift to do the same for you.

If you store packages and valuables, such as cameras in the trunk or on the floor of the car, you won't be tempting petty thieves to break in.

The foregoing might sound like a lot of dos and don'ts, but police investigators find that, when crimes occur, these precautions have often not been taken. It might also sound as if we live under constant threat, but this isn't true. Most people, including strangers, are friendly and trustworthy. So we don't need to be paranoid, but we do need to be prudent.

#25

Preventing Car Theft

There's good news and bad news about preventing vehicle theft. The bad news is that if a skilled professional thief is determined to steal your car, it will happen. There's no way to stop him, despite the extravagant claims of security device manufacturers. The good news is that not that many car thieves are skilled professionals and a few measures will drastically reduce your risks.

There are basically two kinds of car thieves. One is the amateur, a culprit who temporarily takes a car either for joyriding or for committing some other crime. The vehicle is usually then abandoned. (Around half of the vehicles stolen are found by the authorities and returned to their owners.) The other type are professional thieves who sell the cars outside the state or even outside the country. The cars they steal are also sometimes sold to "chop shops," where the vehicles are totally dismantled and the parts sold off.

Whatever their game is, car thieves, like other criminals, look for easy targets of opportunity. So we seniors need to take the actions that discourage them. Number one, always close and lock all doors and windows and take the keys with you. And don't hide an extra key somewhere on the body of the car—thieves always seem to find these. Also, never store your proof of ownership (pink slip) inside your car. Number two, always park in a well-lighted, populated area, preferably where there's some supervision. These two steps will go far in stopping the amateurs.

One of the easiest, most effective ways to prevent your car from being driven off is to learn to lift the distributor cap and take out the rotor. Even if you are all thumbs, any mechanically inclined friend can show you how to do this. The odds that a thief would have a rotor to fit your make of car are one in a million. You just replace the rotor when you're ready to drive again.

Measure number three is to have some sort of alarm or theft deterrent, such as an ignition disabler switch. Like home security systems, all these devices keep coming down in price and becoming more reliable. The various theft prevention items are far from foolproof; I've seen a demonstration where police officers foiled most of them. And they are only an addition, not a substitute for the other security measures. But they're some discouragement to amateurs and pros alike.

Unless you own a highly prized make and model, it's foolish to spend a fortune on security devices because either a more modest system will be effective—or nothing will. Again, comparison shop. You can often find comparable items at half the price in discount auto stores. A basic alarm system runs about $150 and suppliers will usually install them for a reasonable fee. Units include a circuitry sensor that sets off the alarm if any part of the car is opened and a motion sensor that also sets off the alarm if the car is moved or tampered with. You can get a "panic button" key chain with which you can set off the alarm if you run into trouble while leaving or approaching the car. It works on the same principle as a remote TV tuner. Many additional devices are available, such as starter disablers, steering wheel locks, wheel locks, and gas cap locks. You can even buy a "decoy" alarm indicator for $20 that gives your car the appearance of being alarm protected. Look over the gadgets, take your time, don't overbuy, and be skeptical of all salespeoples' claims.

Some security salespeople are semicriminal themselves because they prey upon peoples' fears to hawk shoddy merchandise at inflated prices. These devices will usually be less effective than the manufacturers claim, yet any of them are probably better than nothing at all.

Many petty criminals are not up to stealing cars, but they will break into them to snatch expensive items, such as tape decks, CB radios, cameras, or packages. This is one reason to put your purchases out of sight in the trunk or on the floor. You can also buy locking devices for tape decks that are somewhat effective.

The best evidence that all these devices can have some value as deterrents is that insurance companies, who live by numbers, are now offering discounts if you install them.

#26

Using Public
Transportation Safely

Mass transport can be a good deal even if you drive. The cost may be less than parking fees, especially with senior discount fares, and you can relax and avoid the hassles of navigating traffic. On the downside, there are some crime risks that need attending to. There are snatch-and-run thieveries, harassments and assaults from rowdies, and the chance of getting lost in an unfamiliar, high-crime area. With cabs there is the possibility of getting ripped off by being taken by way of roundabout routes.

Everyone, including the author, who has used public transportation has probably gone astray at some time and ended up in unknown territory. My best bet has always been to immediately get ahold of the transport employees to get straightened out. Failing this, I've asked people who looked to be veteran riders, and they've usually been able to help me. When the areas have been scary, I've taken pains to stay where there are plenty of lights and people.

I've found (the hard way) that what works best is to call the local transit company before I go, get all the details for my route, write them down, and then carry the written details.

Seniors are often targeted on public transportation because thieves feel older people will be less likely to struggle or chase after them. Purses, packages, briefcases, and cameras are what culprits go for, although some will even attempt to snatch watches or other jewelry off a person's body. Their favorite tactic is to grab something and dash out the back exit or strike while their victim is preoccupied with getting off or fumbling with the fare.

Be alert boarding and leaving the conveyance and always have your fare ready beforehand. Stay away from the back exits or empty subway cars. Locate yourself near the driver or conductor if possible. On bus, train, or subway, seat yourself in sections with respectable-looking adults (the strength in numbers principle). If possible, don't take a purse; have your wallet in your jacket pocket. And take no more cash and credit cards than you'll need, including a bit of emergency money. Try not to use isolated stops, especially during off-hours.

Keep any purses, packages, or briefcases in your lap with your hand on them. And stay alert to your surroundings so you are less inviting as a target.

If rowdiness erupts, strive to stay out of it; move away if possible. If you are teased or insulted, don't pick up the gauntlet. Stay coolheaded and ignore it.

When using a cab, ask for an estimate of what the fare will be when you call the dispatcher or first get in. If the actual fare is excessive, get the cab number and the approximate time, and call the cab company immediately. They'll reimburse you and discipline the driver in most cases.

If you are coming in from out of town, inquire beforehand about limousine or shuttle services, which are far cheaper than cabs.

#27

What to Do If You Get Stranded

It can happen to anyone and has happened to most of us. You come out of a movie and your car won't start; your ride never shows up; your car breaks down on the freeway or in an unfamiliar downtown district; you miss your stop on mass transit. You get stranded somewhere. What now?

Whatever the situation, take a few deep calming breaths, look around your immediate surroundings, and assess your options—which are always more than you might at first think. Here's something to keep firmly in mind. Even in unfamiliar high-crime locales there will virtually always be safe havens you can easily reach. And even late at night on a lonely highway, the police or highway patrol are likely to come by before too long. There's much more help available than harm—your task is just to connect with it while staying safe.

- If you're with someone, stay together. For instance, don't leave grandchildren or a spouse alone while you go for help. You can provide each other protection, ideas, and emotional support; and two or more are always safer than one.

- If you've just left some office or entertainment place and your car won't start, go back inside and ask or phone for assistance. Don't accept aid from unidentified people who suddenly appear and offer, because crooks sometimes deliberately disable vehicles.
- If you are alone without a vehicle, look around and spot safe places where there are other people and a phone. Even on "mean streets" there are almost always liquor stores, a cafe, an office building with a security booth, an apartment complex with a guard, a gas station, or a convenience store. Any one of these can provide security and the chance to contact others for help.
- If you are stranded in a vehicle, the highway patrol recommends using your vehicle as your sanctuary until help arrives. If you see a cab, or a maintenance or utility truck, ask them to contact their central dispatcher to call for help. Accept help only from authorized persons.

  Immediately turn on your hazard lights, get out of the line of traffic, and double-check that all doors and windows are secured. Raise the hood and tie a white cloth to it, which is now a widely recognized distress signal. If you have a CB or car phone, call both your auto club and the highway patrol, or the police if you are in town. (It's a good idea to tape these numbers to your instrument.) Some robbers cruise the highways posing as mechanics, so be inflexible about keeping yourself secured. If you are out of your car for any reason and another vehicle begins to stop, get back in your car and secure it.
- It's a wise idea to routinely carry a kit of emergency items in your vehicle. You can get one ready-made from

discount auto stores for about thirty dollars or assemble your own. Include a flashlight, sealed water bottle, tin of cookies or other nonperishable "trail" food, first-aid kit, piece of white cloth, blanket, and essential tools.

* Also consider joining an auto club and keep its number plus other numbers you might need with you. Lots of seniors never get around to doing this; then one day they wish they had.

* If you come across people you don't know with car trouble while you're driving, don't leave your car. Roll your window down only a couple of inches to speak to them and offer only to call the police or their auto club for them. Staged car trouble is becoming a common trick of highway thieves—don't fall for it. Any police officer can tell you tragic stories about well-meaning seniors who got out to help apparently stranded motorists or who picked up what appeared to be a college kid thumbing a ride.

You can survive being stranded. Almost all of us have.

#28

Avoiding Purse Snatchers and Pickpockets

Being around lots of people is a very effective deterrent for most types of crime. Yet there is one kind of criminal who thrives in crowded settings—the pickpocket and purse snatcher. Purse snatchers are often thugs who yank the purse one way while they shove the victim the other to break the strap. Pickpockets are usually more highly skilled and they often work in teams. One attracts your attention while the other lifts your wallet. Not infrequently, the one who distracts you is a child. Pickpockets almost never physically harm their victims, but snatchers will sometimes knock their victims down or break their arms in the process of pulling the purse free. They will also sometimes tear chains and pendants off their targets. Both pickpockets and snatchers quickly fade into the crowd after they strike, so catching them or even identifying them is usually extremely difficult.

Many senior women are now adopting the defensive habit of not even carrying a purse most of the time. They carry a small wallet inside their jackets, sometimes even in hidden pockets they've sewn themselves. Many older men have also quit carrying briefcases or bags. A few seniors have even taken to wearing money belts or ankle pouches. These are all good ideas.

If you do take a purse, it's best to have one with a long strap, not a short handle. The best way to carry it is with the strap over your shoulder, crossing your chest, the purse between your arm and your side, with your hand on it. Never carry it swinging free from your hand or wrist. It's also important to keep the flap or zipper closed so no one can easily reach inside, grab your wallet, and run. Never get a purse with simply a snap closure. Always look for one with a strong zipper. If you're a man, it is safer to carry your wallet in a front or inside jacket pocket than a back pocket.

Crowded malls, crowds at public events such as baseball games, and crowded public transport are the most risky, but these crimes can happen anywhere. If you put your hand on your wallet for some reason, keep it there until you're clear of the foot traffic. If you are bumped in a crowd, immediately focus on your purse or wallet, not on the possibly staged distraction.

Try to refrain from getting loaded down with packages, purses, umbrellas, and such to the point that your hands and arms are filled. Consider taking along a large shopping bag with handles when you plan on doing much shopping so that you're less encumbered and less vulnerable. Also, if you carry little cash and only one credit card you have less to lose.

#29

Dealing with Muggings and Holdups

Muggings are very much a big city crime and not much of a problem in small towns or rural areas. Within cities, they are most likely to occur in the downtown and high-crime districts. Young people are most frequently victimized, but all age groups including seniors are at some risk. Interviews with muggers reveal that they look for easy marks—loners, the intoxicated, and people in places away from public view. Over half the perpetrators are under the influence of drugs or alcohol when they commit their crimes.

Muggers take approximately seven seconds to size up their potential victims. They tend to pass by anyone who looks alert and is walking with a purposeful stride. Most street criminals are not interested in hurting you—but they are entirely willing to meet resistance with force.

In almost all cases, muggers are only interested in quickly getting your money and valuables. They are not moved to mercy by arguments, lectures, or emotional pleas, and they've been known to hurt victims who try such futile tactics. Muggers generally do not physically harm victims who cooperate with their demands.

Traveling in the company of others, staying in public view, and staying out of the worst crime areas will drastically reduce your risks of being mugged—but not entirely eliminate them. If you're confronted by a mugger, surrender your valuables immediately, with no unnecessary conversation or gestures. Muggers want to be quick and get away, so help them do so. Never berate or insult muggers—their behavior is too unpredictable and you risk real injury.

If the mugger is armed with a gun or knife, or if there is more than one of them, resistance is obviously foolish. If the assailant is unarmed, resistance can also be foolish—even when you "win" the scuffle you might well be badly injured in the process. Criminologist John Conklin found that resisting unarmed muggers was the situation in which victims were most likely to be physically injured.

The average mugging lasts less than two minutes, so try to stay coolheaded and weather it, as frightening as the experience may be.

Report any such robbery to the police with as many details as possible—a "trivial" detail often cracks a case. Don't expect the culprit to necessarily be caught this time. But criminals usually operate according to patterns, and the more data the police have, the quicker they can map the offender's pattern and take him down.

In the mugging cases I've studied, the most common mistake seniors made was just to presume they were somehow safe, so they failed to practice such basic protective measures as staying in well-peopled spots.

All crime prevention experts recommend that if you are in a public establishment when a holdup happens, do what the robbers say, don't argue, chatter, or think about being a hero. You are probably facing nervous, desperate, high-strung culprits, so don't push their buttons in any way. Anything you do besides what the criminals want is an added risk for everyone. Again, in virtually all cases, the robbers just want to do their thing and get away quickly—so don't impede them.

In both street muggings and store holdups, concentrate on cutting your losses and surviving the incident intact.

#30

Surviving Street Violence

Stories about drive-by shootings, gang wars, crazed gunmen opening fire on bystanders, and urban riots often seem to dominate the news these days. Luckily, such incidents are actually rare in most low-crime locales, yet they do happen. Even if you run into them, however, your own actions can make all the difference. Your basic aim is to separate yourself as much as possible from the eruption of any violence—just moving away increases your security exponentially.

If you see one or more persons acting erratically, do whatever you can to move away from them—even a few feet further away makes you far safer. If you are walking, turn around and go the other way, go into a building, or cross the street. If you are driving, immediately take any actions that will get you away. This is more important than getting to your original destination. On the highway, slow down and let them get far ahead of you. In town, turn around or at least stop so you're not driving toward the disturbance. Don't presume that the people involved in the disturbance are rational or under any self-control. The perpetrator(s) may be in a killing rage or out of their minds on drugs, and even the bystanders may have become hysterical. The fact that you are an innocent bystander gives you little or no protection.

If gunfire erupts anywhere near you, never stand up and crane your neck or go see what's happening. There are two main tactics to improve survival odds that have been practiced by military forces since the beginning of time:

1. ***Move away if you can.*** The nature of firearm ballistics is that if you double your distance from the point of attack you are roughly four times as safe. Also, put any barriers, such as a thick wall, between yourself and the disturbance.

2. ***Drop to the ground or floor.*** Your clothes or your dignity should be the least of your worries. Dropping down and staying down increases your security manyfold, as any combat veteran can tell you. On the ground you are only a fraction of the target you are when sitting up or standing, whether the bullets are aimed at you or are stray ricochets. Even when you're at home, if you hear gunfire stay low and move to the other side of your dwelling. With the tremendous penetrating power of modern weapons it's neither safe nor wise to peer out your windows.

If you see a brawl break out between adults, the police advise that you stay clear of it and call them. If you encounter a woman or child being beaten, you'll have to decide, by weighing the circumstances and your own moral and practical considerations, whether to interfere or call the police.

Most people can and do survive random violence, even full-blown civil disruptions, and you can, too.

#31
Avoiding Rape

The risk of a woman being sexually assaulted falls off sharply after age thirty, partly because older women have a lot more crime avoidance savvy than young girls. For instance, they are far less likely to get drunk and go off somewhere private with a virtual stranger. Yet there are rape cases involving even women in their eighties, so the risk is never entirely left behind. Happily, all the tactics of household security and going out safely mentioned earlier act as effective countermeasures for most types of crime, including rape. Rape counselors have additional advice to increase security. (Men should know about this, too, to help protect the women in their lives.) Perhaps the most basic point is that a woman has to be her own chaperone and security officer. No, this isn't fair, but it's a fact of life at present.

Women the world over are in a double bind. They are pressured from infancy to look, feel, and smell attractive. Yet if they do so they make themselves targets of sexual assaults and harassments. And because rape virtually always involves power and punishment motivations, even women who don't make themselves attractive can be victims. So you are not totally free of risk because you are a senior now or you consider yourself "unattractive."

There are three high-risk factors: (1) being alone, (2) being isolated from public view, and (3) being vulnerable to the assailant. All three factors are almost always present in a rape case. Change any one of them and rape is almost certainly avoided.

Always venturing out with a companion is the best single countermeasure against rape, but this isn't always possible. Even if you can't be with others, strive to be *around* others and you'll have almost the same level of protection. If you can't be with someone or around others, at least stay in public view. For instance, stay on well-traveled streets or ask a security officer to watch that you get safely to your car. Most rapists won't chance situations where they are likely to be seen and recognized.

Don't be alone or in an isolated situation with potential rapists—which for senior women means unidentified strangers. Date rape, so rampant among teenage girls, is quite uncommon among senior women. But you'd probably be surprised if you added up the number of males you come into casual contact with every month, in circumstances where you know little or nothing about them or their true intentions. (Some of these may have not rape, but emotional or physical seduction followed by exploitation in mind.) You don't need to treat them all as "guilty until proven innocent," but do treat them as question marks until you've discovered who they are and what their game is.

When you meet a male you are not acquainted with, for business or social reasons, do so in the company of others or at least under supervised conditions or in a public place. Have a friend or neighbor over if someone you don't yet know is coming to your home. Also, going off alone with someone you just met, even at a church social, is adventuresome at best. Suggest alternatives where you'll remain with those you know, such as a group of you going for coffee. Since time immemorial, women have stayed together for mutual security as well as companionship, and the tactic is as effective today.

Beyond not being alone in isolated situations, rape avoidance involves taking measures to be less accessible to the assailant. So any barrier such as a locked door, any hint of protection such as a barking dog, and any disturbance such as an alarm going off can turn a would-be assailant away.

Extensive studies of convicted rapists show that most of them plan to rape but have no specific woman in mind—they look for women who they can get at and who seem defenseless. They might have passed by many women before choosing the situation and victim that seemed right. Most relied on threats and intimidation to make their victims submit and actually used force only to quell resistance. The majority of the physical injuries to victims were minor and resulted from rough handling. (Over 95 percent of convicted rapists are under forty.)

In the unlikely event that you are confronted by a rapist, what should you do? The answer depends entirely on the situation. No ironclad advice, such as "always resist" or "never resist," can be given. Obviously, you should escape to safety—the safe room in your home or a public place—if possible. If other people are fairly close, scream, yell "fire," set off your personal alarm to attract attention. Make as much of a public disturbance as possible; this destroys the "isolated" factor rapists count on. The assailant may become uncertain and flee, whether anyone comes or not. Rape crisis experts also recommend the tactic of "freaking out"—shrieking, urinating, vomiting, convulsing. This might scare off or turn off the rapist. Pleading is highly questionable; rapists are not noted for their compassion.

If you sense an intruder when alone in your residence, get to a neighbor if you can. If not, barricade yourself in your safe room and make all the noise you can.

Crime experts remain sharply divided over the question of physically resisting a rapist. If an assailant is armed or there's more than one of them, physical resistance might only increase the likelihood of further harm. Likewise if the assailant has a brutal or violent disposition.

Successful unarmed resistance usually requires training and practice, although a woman's rage sometimes supplies enough galvanization. Rape prevention classes and self-defense courses can provide the training on how to incapacitate an attacker.

Any weapon, such as Mace or a gun, has to be *immediately* available at the moment of attack and a person has to be well trained in its use. Again, police have found that some victims had a false sense of security because of having a weapon in their purses, so they neglected the more basic and reliable avoidance procedures.

If rape does happen to you or someone you know, immediately contact your local rape crisis center or women's center. These centers have an outstanding record of support and help. They know what to do with regard to handling medical examinations and police reports. And they will usually supply someone to accompany the rape survivor through these routines. Their knowledge and help provide the vital support a survivor needs.

Despite recent reforms, the criminal justice system is no great shakes either in assisting victims or in prosecuting rape cases. However, the system usually works better in treating the survivor respectfully and bringing the culprit to justice when the woman is a senior.

And yes, there can be life after rape. As one sixty-year-old survivor said, "You don't burn down your house just because some bastard tracks mud into your kitchen." Extensive research has clearly shown that the biggest single factor in successful recovery from rape is support from women's centers, family, and friends. The factors that go into this support include listening; unconditional affection (not pity); not blaming the victim, even indirectly; letting the survivor make her own decisions without "taking over" or giving streams of advice; and helping the person get on with her life.

There *are* advantages to being older. Rape is one of the most uncommon crimes against senior women and almost nonexistent against older men. With precautions, the risks can be reduced almost to the vanishing point.

#32

A Crime-free Workplace

Most seniors still have a paying job or do volunteer work of some sort. Going to work, for pay or charity, is enough of a venture without adding in crime victimization, so it is wise to adopt a few protective routines. This is true even if you are only lending a hand at a local charity or church. There are probably some special circumstances surrounding your own line of work that you need to consider, but here are general security points that apply everywhere.

Your workplace almost certainly has at least some rudimentary security system. Take a bit of time and learn it, including fire alarm locations, emergency exits, and emergency buttons on the elevators. All of these can be adapted for crime thwarting in an emergency. For instance, if you find yourself in trouble, you can always set off a fire alarm and yell "fire" or punch the elevator alarm.

When entering or leaving your workplace, always try to be with other workers, or at least in sight of them, because this is when muggings and other unpleasantries most often occur. Some workers arrange "buddy systems" where two or more people see one another safely to and from their vehicles. If the workplace or building has an escort service, use it. Stay alert for anything out of the ordinary during these transits and act on anything that even *seems* suspicious. A great many older people have followed these routines and have gone for decades with no incidents.

Our lives would be tougher without elevators, yet even veteran police officers approach them alertly. In some locations, elevators are prime places for fast robberies and molestations so it's best to ride them with other workers you know. If you see unfamiliar persons hanging around the elevators, don't get on—and if they get on with you, get off. You can mutter something like: "Hell, I forgot my package," and leave if anyone suspicious gets on while you're riding up or down. It's also a good idea to stand near the control panel so you can push the alarm button.

Modern building codes require that office structures have an extensive system of stairways and exits, which is a mixed blessing crime-wise. These stairwells can be riskier to use than elevators, especially during off-hours or if you are alone. Also, if you need to go into an isolated section of the building while working or volunteering, ask security or at least a coworker to accompany you. The workplace is a prime area for petty and serious thievery. Your colleagues may be trustworthy, but there may be a continual stream of clients, service personnel, and visitors, and it is easy for swift-footed crooks to mix in with this traffic.

Secure purses and valuables in a drawer or take them with you even when you just run to the restroom or out for a drink of water. I know of several cases where purses, and even computers, were snatched from offices when the occupant only stepped down the hall "for just a minute." With the maze of exits, floors, and stairwells, it's easy for nimble culprits to get away.

Even items like radios left out overnight at workplaces may disappear, so lock them away.

Be especially security-conscious when you have to be in a workplace during off-hours, while few people are around. These are the times when burglaries, robberies, and assaults are more likely to happen. Insist that there are adequate security measures, let building security know you are there, and ask them or a coworker to accompany you about the building. Keep your own area locked and don't casually allow anyone in that you don't personally know without checking them out with security. If you notice or feel anything is suspicious, alert security; don't shrug it off as the willies. When working late or working alone on the weekends it might also be prudent to call a cab to take you home.

With a bit of prodding, management is usually willing to upgrade worker and volunteer security. The electronics revolution has made it possible to have TV security monitoring and workers supplied with beepers or panic buttons. But whatever the setup, continue to be your own guardian.

There's another important aspect to crime avoidance on the job which is too often overlooked. *Getting along* can be at least as important as keeping track of your purse or wallet. Try to keep relations as harmonious as possible with all those you come into contact with on the job. If you needlessly antagonize the other people connected with your work, they'll take it personally. Aside from making the workplace more tense and unpleasant, this ill will can burst forth in actions ranging from petty vandalism to, in extreme cases, homicide. Research has shown that there is frequently a "get even" aspect to many burglaries, robberies, assaults, and rapes.

For example, in his research with inmates, ex-superthief Jack Maclean found that one out of every twelve burglaries had a revenge component.

You don't have to be a pushover or a Pollyanna in order to get along well. You can disagree with others, voice your own opinions, and stand up for your rights—just strive to do so diplomatically and in a friendly fashion. There's probably nobody alive who can get along with everybody, but the more people you have in your corner, the more allies you have in good times or emergencies. A considerate attitude and a mild show of fellowship will go a long way. If you find yourself being gruff, psychological research shows that if you offer some explanation such as, "Sorry, I didn't get any sleep last night," the other person isn't likely to hold a grudge and may even become sympathetic. These "getting along" pointers are good advice in all situations, not just the workplace.

Unfriendly coworkers, bosses, and clients can be a source of crime; friendly ones are a bulwark against it.

Incidentally, an extensive National Institutes of Health study found that work satisfaction is the biggest single factor in longevity.

#33

Protection During Hospital Stays

Seniors spend more time in hospitals than younger people. During their stays, they should be able to concentrate on getting better without worrying about theft or about victimization by the hospital's procedures and personnel. A twenty-year veteran nurse supervisor once told me, "People think hospitals are safe places, but they are really very dangerous places." Luckily, a few guidelines can help minimize such dangers.

Don't go into a hospital unless you really need to. If a doctor recommends elective surgery, get a second, *independent* opinion—not just from the doctor's crony down the hall. Also, many surgical procedures can now be done on an outpatient basis, so check on this possibility. At the very least, you'll save money and inconvenience. (Hospital stays always seem to involve some unplanned personal expenses.)

Leave excess cash, jewelry, and other valuables at home. (But take enough cash to get a cab home.) If you are hospitalized because of an emergency, get your excess money, credit cards, jewelry, and rings placed in the hospital vault. When such items are unsecured, thievery is quite common. Most hospitals provide sealable security envelopes for this. Have your envelope signed for by a hospital representative.

Hospitals often have sprawling parking lots and secluded corridors, with lots of unidentified people coming and going at all hours. So follow the security tips from earlier entries when arriving, leaving, or moving about the premises.

Emergency rooms, especially on nights and weekends, are often full of people involved with drugs and violence. If you are waiting in the ER, don't get involved in any arguments or disputes and quietly move away from any erupting incidents. Some ER patients are brought in against their will by family or the police and are not rational. So just steer clear and let the staff handle any problems.

Ask for generic drugs during and after your stay. Most of them are made by the same major pharmaceutical companies that make the name brands, and they often cost only half as much or less.

Hospital personnel sometimes display a rigid "I know best" attitude toward patients, discouraging questions and insisting on compliance with their instructions. This can be hazardous to your health. Bernie Siegel, the great humanist-doctor, recommends being an assertive, questioning, even troublesome patient. *Never lose sight of the fact that it is your body and your life.*

Know and insist upon your Patients' Rights. Most states and modern countries have now passed some form of these into law to protect patients from exploitation and victimization by the health care industry. Ask for a copy from your doctor or the hospital staff. Better yet, get a copy of the local version from your library or your Area Agency on Aging beforehand. They should, at the minimum, include the following:

- The right to actively participate in all decisions involving your medical care.
- The right to receive adequate information about your illness, proposed treatments, risks, and prognosis for recovery, in understandable terms.
- The right to refuse treatment.
- Privacy and confidentiality of your condition from unauthorized persons.
- The right to leave the hospital, even against your physician's recommendations.
- The right to be told if a proposed treatment is experimental, and the right to refuse to participate in any research project.
- The right to a detailed, itemized billing and the right to question any items. Errors are all too common.
- The right to a living will (discussed in entry #64, "The Right to Live and the Right to Die").
- The extension of all these rights to any person making decisions for the patient.

Even if these points are not yet enacted into law in your locale, insist on them anyway.

Medical and hospital bills are notoriously complicated and untrustworthy—and surprise, surprise, in the majority of cases, the errors are substantial overcharges. I suggest joining the People's Medical Society, 462 Walnut Street, Allentown, PA 18102. The fifteen-dollar annual membership fee includes help decoding your bills and filing complaints.

If you are going into a hospital for a life-threatening condition, I strongly recommend you read Dr. Bernie Siegel's *Peace, Love and Healing*.

#34

Safe Recreational and Sports Activities

While out golfing, playing tennis, attending aerobics classes, swimming, and so on, you are usually quite safe personally if you follow minimal security habits such as staying in sight of others. But there are two main threats: thievery and the covert gleaning of information to be used against you. Often you'll change into special clothing so your wallet or purse (and even the clothes themselves) may be vulnerable. And idle conversation is free-flowing in such settings. Loose lips can provide criminals with tips.

Recreational and sports activities often involve expensive equipment, easily fenced, and thieves know this very well. In fact, some crooks specialize in these kinds of robberies. And the walls (or that quiet attendant) have ears. So some countermeasures make good sense.

* Take little cash and only one credit card with you, so you'll have less to lose.
* Leave expensive watches, rings, and jewelry safely hidden away at home. Wear a ten-dollar watch and costume jewelry with no sentimental value. A fake costume

wedding band instead of your real one isn't a bad idea either.

- If possible, change into your sports clothes before leaving home, so you won't need to use a locker.
- Report to security or the management any suspicious circumstances or persons who "don't seem to belong." This won't always be a successful screening because recreational thieves are often adept at blending in and passing as one of the crowd. But some malefactors are dumb and easily spotted as out of place.
- Keep all your equipment and valuables with you or safely locked away in the facilities provided.
- Be circumspect in what you tell other participants about yourself. Don't boast about a valuable coin or gun collection or freely give out the details of your daily life or a trip you are planning. If you speak so openly about yourself and your possessions, nothing will come of it forty-nine times out of fifty, but why risk it? There are many cases where such overhead information has even been sold by attendants to burglars and swindlers.
- Here's an often overlooked exposure. In parking or making other pickup arrangements, keep in mind how conditions may change by the time you leave. For instance, the spot you park in might be highly visible and in a populated location, but if you leave several hours later, it might be dusk or late at night, and the lot might have become isolated by then. Use a "buddy system" to see that those who remain late get safely to their vehicles, or ask the management to see you to your car. Don't skimp on this one because "nothing ever happens here."
- When you leave, if you have any suspicion that you're

being followed, do not go home. If you're driving, go directly to a police station or public place and get help. If you are on foot, duck into the nearest "safe haven" and, again, ask for help. Being followed is rare for seniors, but it has happened.

* When you get back home from an event, follow the tips in entry #39, "Arriving Back Home Safely."
* If you have any medical condition, it's a good idea to let your recreation companions or the management know and to specify what you want done in case of an emergency.

Millions of older persons enjoy recreational activities every week in perfect safety, and if you follow these and the other tips in this chapter, you can, too.

#35

The Great Outdoors

Recently, more and more seniors have become active in outdoor and wilderness pursuits, such as camping, hiking, and even mountain climbing. The main problem crime-wise is that these activities usually involve being fairly isolated and in unfamiliar territory. Criminality is still fairly rare in most state and national preserves, but it happens often enough that security should be considered.

If you are fairly new at the outdoor activity, an excellent strategy is to go with someone more experienced, who knows the ropes and the lay of the land. Park and wilderness preserve officials are also extremely helpful in tipping you to the safe and dangerous places and practices. It is also wise to let them know the details of your plans. They will often check periodically to see that all is well with you. Even if you are just going off fishing for part of a day, it is a wise move to let a friend and local authorities in that area know. Also, for everyone's sake, report any suspicious persons or incidents to local officials—you might be saving the next person who comes along from grief.

A first-aid kit and vehicle emergency kit are good for both

accidents and protection, since being hurt or stranded makes one more vulnerable to human scavengers. Have a detailed map of the area, too. If you do much wilderness activity, consider getting a CB radio which can quickly put you in touch with help in case of trouble.

A major problem is the security of your vehicle and its contents while you are away in the wilds. Standard locks that come with the vehicle are usually inadequate. If possible, park in a supervised area. Also, see an auto parts store or locksmith to have better locks, door frames, and antitheft devices installed. One very effective tactic you can easily learn is to remove the rotor and take it with you or hide it near the vehicle. Additional locks or tie-downs should be used for valuable contents. Because most crooks don't want to confront groups of people who may be armed, sneak thievery is far more common in the great outdoors than armed robbery.

When shopping for a "wilderness tour" it is wise to work with a well-established travel agency or reputable senior organization, such as the AARP.

#36

Enjoying Secure Holidays

Evidence clearly shows that some kinds of robbery and personal hazard risks increase at holiday times. These are also times when people get into a festive mood and become more careless. Without dampening any holiday spirits, a few important precautions can be taken.

In talking with seniors, I've found that many of them just assumed that crooks took time off and celebrated the holidays like everyone else. In fact, the opposite is true. *Criminals do not take time off during the holidays.*

Christmas

The two crimes that increase around Christmastime are thievery of packages and home burglaries. Thieves know that shoppers will have their arms full of expensive presents and that easily snatched valuables will be gift-wrapped and laid out underneath the trees in people's homes. A convicted burglar remarked, "It was my most productive time; people left their doors open, even notes saying when they'd be back."

If you don't relax your routine security measures, and if

you're a bit more cautious, you'll probably remain in the safety zones. When shopping, don't become overburdened with multiple packages, and don't leave piles of packages visible in your car as you go from place to place. Take along large shopping bags that can hold several items, and as you purchase items, lock them away in your trunk. With expensive purchases, don't hesitate to ask employees to see you to your vehicle. Also, consider doing your Christmas shopping early to avoid both the crowds and the crooks.

Take some extra care to see that your dwelling appears occupied—a radio tuned to Christmas carols, inside lights on, and such. And continue keeping potential entrances locked. Surveys of holiday victims have shown that they were often preoccupied with the bustle of preparations and events, so their guard was down more than usual.

There is also a subtle scam to sidestep during the Christmas season and other holidays. Holiday means *holy day*, yet advertisers and merchants heavily pressure us to overspend and hint that we may be guilty for not doing so. But there's no reason to empty your nest egg for gifts—it is the thought that counts.

New Year's Eve

Driving a vehicle while intoxicated is now a serious crime in most countries of the world and it is the number one menace for anyone who goes out New Year's Eve. At least one-fifth of the motorists you meet on the road will have been drinking and as many as one-tenth will be drunk or stoned to the point that they're a real threat. And the later the hour, the more inebriated drivers there will be. An obvious countermeasure is to stay home, and if you have company over, arrange for them to stay the night. Even if you can hold your liquor, how about all those other guys on the road? This isn't about morality; it's about twisted human wreckage.

If you do go out drinking, be certain to have a designated driver who doesn't imbibe.

Burglary is also a New Year's risk. In fact, the renowned ex-superthief Jack Maclean said it is the busiest night of the year for many burglars. If a dwelling is dark and quiet, thieves know that the occupants will almost certainly be gone until after midnight. And there are usually valuable items laying about because of the holiday season. Again, the best defense if you go out is to make your dwelling appear occupied by using lights and noise.

In recent years a practice has grown up to celebrate New Year's that has become another menace. As the midnight hour approaches, growing numbers of people are firing guns, ostensibly into the air. Old-time cowboys would sometimes "hurrah" a town in similar fashion when they rode in at the end of a long cattle drive, and not a few townspeople got injured.

Discharging weapons within city limits is a crime almost everywhere, and police have been issuing strict warnings about this New Year's practice, but they've been unable to curb it. A main problem is that so many modern weapons carry long distances and have high penetrating power. Your best bet, if you are in an area where this practice occurs, is to stay away from windows and doorways as Auld Lang Syne approaches.

Fourth of July

If crooks see a dark, quiet house on the Fourth of July evening, they figure no one will be back until after the fireworks and they think break-in. If it's a hot summer night and some windows are also left open for ventilation, their mouths probably start watering. So again, take a few minutes to ensure that your home appears secure and occupied to outsiders before you go out. The Fourth is also the other holiday when the nasty habit of firing weapons after dark has become fairly widespread, so take extra precautions.

Halloween

Malicious mischief and vandalism are the main crime problems for seniors during Halloween. Youths dressed up as ghouls and goblins sometimes feel they need to act out the part. You may have even taken part in some of these activities yourself when you were younger.

Check over your home's exterior grounds with an eye to minimizing temptations. Store away all garden tools, portable lawn furniture and equipment, benches and ladders, barbecue grills, and so on. If you have some place to lock up garbage cans, that's a good idea, too. If you have a garage, park your car inside and lock both the car and the garage. If you don't have garage facilities, lock up the car and park it in a well-lighted place that isn't secluded. Light up your property well, especially the sides and back, and suggest that your neighbors do the same. These measures will discourage vandals and also make it safer for the trick-or-treaters.

It is a good idea to scan trick-or-treaters through your front door's peephole and avoid opening for older kids if you don't know them. You might just say you're out of treats loudly through the door if the callers rouse your suspicions.

Special Occasions

By now it should be clear that special occasions can involve special risks. When you have parties or family get-togethers in your home, the main crime exposure is the heisting of loose money and small valuables. Nowadays these gatherings often include stepchildren and stepgrandchildren, new romantic partners of friends—people you may not know very well. Such relative strangers are the most common culprits, although your precious grandkids can have sticky fingers, too.

Before the guests arrive, take a few minutes to look over all the rooms of your house. You might be surprised at how many small valuables you have lying around in plain sight—earrings, rings, watches, silver knick-knacks, a gold chain, or a small camera. Put them away. Also, see that any diary, journal, or private letters and financial statements are not available to curious eyes.

Have a thought also to protecting your guests' purses and coats if there are lots of people, including ones you don't know well. Establish a safe place where the items are not likely to be rifled through.

Both weddings and funerals are usually announced in local newspapers and various sorts of tradespeople are also usually involved with them. So they are widely known special events. Some burglars scan the papers for special events; they know all members of the family's dwelling will be attending and lay their own plans accordingly. If you are attending a wedding or funeral, arrange to have a friend stay at your house during the ceremonies if possible. Or at least get one or more people from your neighborhood network to keep an eye on your place.

There is a different kind of criminality to be on guard against around weddings and funerals. Some unscrupulous tradespeople will use the occasion of joy or mourning to pressure the participants into overspending, sometimes for shoddy goods at inflated prices. People who are ordinarily savvy consumers can be caught up in the emotions of the event and fall for these scams.

Whatever is happening with your heart during holidays and special occasions, keep your head about maintaining security and you'll probably remain crime-free.

#37

Traveling Smart

If you're going on a trip, you don't need to sneak out of town, but there's no reason to widely advertise the fact either. Crooks have eyes and ears, so don't tip them off.

For home protection while you are away, the basic strategy is to arrange things so your dwelling doesn't look any different than usual. If you are retired and around the house a lot this is particularly important because otherwise your absence will be more conspicuous.

What are the obvious signs that you are gone for a while? Several days worth of newspapers piled up on the lawn, an overstuffed mailbox, a house that remains dark and quiet where usually there were lights and noise, all the curtains drawn when they weren't before, and an unanswered ringing telephone.

Each of these "nobody home" signs can be neutralized. Ask someone trustworthy from your neighborhood network to pick up your newspapers off the lawn, your mail and packages and any other deliveries, and also see that the grounds don't become unkempt. Do not notify everyone to have all deliveries stopped, because this broadcasts your absence too widely and there are now too many cases of even postal employees tipping off their unsavory friends. However, do let your local police know you'll be gone or the management and security if you live in a housing complex. Get several inexpensive timers to turn inside lights, radios, or TV sets on and off at different times. You can also get a couple of photoelectric sockets that will turn a couple more interior lights on at dusk and off at dawn—you just plug them into a wall socket, then plug your light into them. Turn the bell down on your phone so people outside can't hear its ringing. And arrange curtains and drapes as usual. In the time period before you leave, you might start closing curtains to obscure portions of your dwelling; then nothing would change when you go. If you haven't yet gotten around to creatively hiding away your small valuables or putting them in a safe-deposit box, before you go would be an excellent time to do so. Just prior to leaving, do a final check that your home security measures are in place.

Travel "bargain" scams are rampant these days, so make your arrangements or reservations only through established, reputable travel agencies. There are many legitimate bargains—senior discounts, discount tours, off-season rates at hotels and resorts—so don't overpay for transportation or accommodations.

However you are traveling, know your route beforehand, so you don't get stranded in unknown situations and places where you'd be more vulnerable to mischief. If you are driving, most auto clubs provide route-mapping services free of charge, or you can buy an inexpensive travel guide. If you are going by plane, train, or bus, your travel agent can help. One big advantage of group tours is that these details are handled for you.

If you'll be driving, it is wise to have a full twelve-point maintenance checkup and tune-up done on your vehicle to help prevent breakdowns, on-the-road vulnerability, and out-of-town repair ripoffs.

If you travel by air or other public conveyance, take as little luggage as possible so you have less to keep track of. I always try to stuff everything into a carryon. And keep your luggage close to you, since it is a prime target for thieves. Consider using scruffy, inexpensive luggage because it is far less tempting to robbers. Upon arriving, go to baggage claims right away—a routine practice of airport thieves is to grab luggage that goes around the carousel more than twice.

Studies of terminal baggage thieves have found that they often work in teams, scan hundreds of passengers, signal each other, and move off from people who seem alert. When they strike, one will usually distract the victim while the other grabs and runs. Or they'll wait until a victim steps up to the ticket counter, then slip away with a bag. A good protective tactic is to use curbside baggage check-in. And when greeting long-lost friends, don't neglect your luggage even for a minute.

Most hotels and motels are fairly secure as long as a person uses common sense and the security routines outlined throughout this book. An unknown number of persons may have room keys, so use the deadbolts and chains as well as the standard lock when you are in the room. And don't leave valuables lying out in plain sight, even when just going to the bathroom. A good idea is to store them in the hotel safe and get a receipt. More and more hotels are converting to electronic card locks and installing peepholes in the doors, which is a much safer setup. Because of several recent lawsuits, hotel and motel management are eager to avoid incidents, so you can almost always count on their help in case of trouble.

All experts recommend using credit cards and traveler's checks as much as possible and carrying a minimum of cash. Split up what cash you have and carry it in several places.

Stay alert in the elevators and hallways and shun secluded sections of the buildings and grounds. Use your common sense in interacting with strangers. If you are alone, ask security or a bellboy to accompany you to your room, and have them wait until you have safely entered.

When traveling, it's good to keep a couple of things in mind. One is that you won't be on your familiar home turf. Things, including the local crime situation, may be subtly different even in another part of your home state. The area might be safer than you're used to, but it's prudent to ask the locals for instance, about where to go and not to go. I've found desk clerks, coffee shop workers, and even pedestrians to be very helpful in scouting the local scene. The laws, the "way things are done," and the kinds of crime risks vary from place to place. As two examples, gun laws and intoxicated driving laws vary enormously from place to place.

The other thing is that criminals prefer to hit on out-of-state travelers for a good reason. Most travelers are unable or unwilling to go through all the complications, inconvenience, and expense involved with coming back, perhaps many times, to help prosecute the culprits.

While traveling usually involves unfamiliar situations, your own good sense and these simple security steps will protect you.

#38

Tips for Secure Foreign Travel

Ever-increasing numbers of seniors are becoming worldwide travelers. In response to this trend, travel experts, crime experts, and governments are issuing advisories on how to travel safely to foreign places. Their tips are based on the real-life experiences of successful and unsuccessful trekkers. As far as we know, travel risks aren't any greater for seniors— but they aren't any fewer.

Newspaper headlines demonstrate how unsettled many parts of the world are today. So always check on the stability of current conditions in the places you are planning to visit. Check with a travel agency and your government to see if there are any travel advisories. In the United States the State Department issues such bulletins. Most industrialized nations are fairly safe, but Third World countries can be tinderboxes. Checking it out will help prevent you from innocently arriving in the midst of civil strife.

Foreign travel scams are rampant, yet there are real bargains to reward the patient searcher. The two safest bets are an established travel agency or group tours organized by a local senior club, church, or other recognized organization.

Tell an agent explicitly that you're looking for bargains, and check the agency out with the Better Business Bureau or its equivalent in your country.

Most countries and local areas put out beautiful brochures that may have little to do with reality. These are advertisements, not fact booklets. (This is also true of retirement community promotions.) It is wise to do a little homework on your own. Use the *Reader's Guide to Periodical Literature* at your local library to read some recent articles on your destination, and get a recent book by a travel journalist or an up-to-date guidebook on the area. Your librarian or bookseller can help you find the best ones. If possible, talk with people who have recently been there. You don't have to become an expert, but it's good to get some preliminary notions about current conditions, customs, taboos, and so on.

Tourism is a major industry in many parts of the world, and the money tourists spend is welcome virtually everywhere. But criminals are happy to see the tourists arrive, too, and there is at least a small criminal element wherever you go. From their viewpoint, it's open season on tourists. The two main threats are local versions of thefts and frauds. Nimble thieves who snatch purses, cameras, jewelry, or tote bags, and then disappear down a maze of native streets are a common problem. Local "bargains" in jewelry, rugs and clothing, artifacts and relics are also a common fraudulent industry. (In one common trick, they let you bargain them down to a price that is twice what the item is actually worth.) Unfortunately, such petty thefts and frauds are rampant throughout the world. Local governments, mindful of tourist money, do strive to curb more serious crimes, such as armed robberies, assaults, or kidnappings, but these do sometimes happen.

When going abroad it is wise to redouble all your security routines—stay around people and in public view, keep your belongings in hand or safely locked away, secure your lodgings, and be cautious about unidentified strangers. Also, ask your tour guide, travel agent, and lodgings personnel what to watch out for. There might be recent developments or a new local fashion in crime you need to know about. In every clime, some situations and places are dangerous and some are safe.

There is a vital fact about foreign travel that many people, old or young, don't realize. *When you are in a foreign country you are subject to their laws.* Only government officials have diplomatic immunity. Ask what is illegal in the place you are planning to visit and then refrain from doing it. If you get into legal trouble, your own consulate can often do very little to help you. The local justice system can be barbaric and the local jails stark and grim by your standards. Local governments do extend a bit of leniency toward foreigners, but this only goes so far and corrupt local officers may be living well off bribes and extortions from travelers. As one example of legal differences, drunk driving penalties are often shockingly severe.

When you go to a foreign country, you are plunging into a different culture with different beliefs and customs. The crime scene will be different, too. But the same bottom-line thwarting tactics can be applied to put all the odds in your favor.

#39

Arriving Back Home Safely

Most of us come back a bit weary from our travels. Whether you have been gone an hour or a month, you want to get inside your dwelling, kick off your shoes with a sigh of relief, and get comfortable. But the arrival period involves increased exposure, so it isn't time to let down your guard quite yet.

As you approach your dwelling, look to see that no unidentified people are loitering around the entrance. If they are, don't leave the safety of your car. You might roll your window down no more than an inch and ask loudly, "Can I help you?" If in *any* doubt, drive off to the safety of a neighbor and call for help. If someone else drives you home, ask them to wait until you've safely entered and wave an okay to them from a window. (Do the same for anyone you give a lift to.) If you live in a housing complex and see unidentified loiterers around your own entrance, back away and find the manager or go to a neighbor's place.

From your prior security measures, you should have a clear, well-lighted view of your entrance. If there are even slight signs of a break-in, do not enter. Go instead to a trusted neighbor or nearby public phone and call the police.

Your first impulse might be to rush inside, but you want to avoid any possible confrontation with intruders who might still be present. They can easily become desperate and vicious, like cornered animals. Never try to block the exit of a fleeing culprit. Chasing after them is strictly police business.

Have your keys in hand as you approach your door so you don't have to remain outside fumbling for them.

If you are approached by anyone, do not start to open your door while answering their questions. "Push-in" crimes, where a culprit shoves you into your dwelling and follows you in, are on the increase, especially in multiple-dwelling complexes. Preliminary evidence shows that seniors, especially women, are the most likely push-in targets. If you can, leave the area and return with help. If the person is menacing, try to trip a fire alarm and yell "fire," or use your panic button to set off your own alarm. If the situation turns into a robbery, surrender your valuables but *don't unlock your door.* You are less at risk in the hallway or at your front door than inside your dwelling. With some cash or valuables, the culprit will almost always just flee.

Once you are safely inside, check that you've taken the keys out of the lock, then relock your door from the inside. A surprising number of people often forget and leave their keys sticking in the outside door—the author has done it several times. So take a moment to see that you have your keys, your door is secured, and all is well.

Now you can relax.

❖ FOUR ❖

Dodging Swindles and Consumer Frauds

Swindles and consumer frauds are the crimes most frequently committed against seniors. Unfortunately, such crimes are currently a growth industry. The U.S. Department of Justice has estimated that the annual cost of scams and corporate crimes is eighteen times the cost of all street crimes combined. And the odds that we will be defrauded this year, at least for a few dollars, are far greater than the odds that we'll be mugged or burglarized.

Older people are the prime targets for scams because they have a lot more property and resources. It would take a large book to describe all the swindles being worked on seniors, and the book would need constant updating as new scams emerged. But the good news is that all swindlers operate in similar basic ways.

In the entries in this chapter, I've culled some of the most effective countermeasures.

#40

How Swindlers Operate—and How to Thwart Them

Self-improvement workshop leaders report that participants are usually quite willing to talk openly about their love lives but clam up about their financial affairs—with good reason. There are literally millions of people who want your money. Some of them will give you something in return—we call these businesspeople and professionals. Others aim to rip you off—we call them criminals. Sometimes the line between the two is very blurred.

Everywhere we turn these days, new consumer frauds, con games, corporate corruptions, and malpractice by professionals are uncovered. There are always some risks involved in any kind of purchase or investment. Also, there are always risks involved when we rely on the judgment of professionals such as doctors, lawyers, and financial advisers, no matter how legitimate and well meaning they are. And there is the possibility of fraud in every human activity, from going on a date to investing your life savings. But the charlatans give us no chance at all.

Older people are actually less easily hoodwinked than the young because we are less suggestible. But, we are mostly on

131

our own because there is no way regulatory agencies can protect us from all the schemers.

In this entry, I will sketch how all charlatans work and give you some generic countermeasures to take against them. Thwarting tactics for specific kinds of scams are then addressed in the rest of the chapter. *The first rule is never to make an exception to these guidelines.*

There's an old saying that the world's financial markets are fueled by two fundamental forces: greed and fear. Well, the same two forces lie at the bottom of most scams and professional ripoffs. We are all a bit fearful about some things, such as our health and financial security, and we can be made more so by clever "fear merchant" manipulators. Most of us are also a bit greedy; after working hard and paying our dues, the idea of some easy windfall is surely enticing. Charlatans know these facts of human nature very well and use them against us to reap *their* windfalls. They are also adept at playing upon our naivete and gullibility.

Their schemes rely upon all the tricks of persuasion, public relations, advertising, and seduction. Their come-ons and offers are usually extremely clever, and they display a level of creative truth-twisting that would do credit to a politician's speechwriter. Swindlers also keep abreast of current events and weave half-truths about them into their pitches. One could almost admire their artistry, if it weren't for their despicable purposes. Sometimes they employ subtle word manipulations to stay just inside the letter of the law, while fracturing its spirit.

Phrases such as "you have been specially selected" only mean that someone bought a mailing list you were on. These lists are sold back and forth across the country, and you can get on them just by subscribing to a magazine. "You have won a prize" is no prize at all if you have to send money or call a 900 number and pay by the minute to listen to their spiel. Phone, mail, and in-person frauds should truly read: "Congratulations! You have been selected to receive a fleecing." (Legitimate contests and sweepstakes never charge you or require expensive toll calls.)

In some scams you get a *little* something for your money—worn circulated coins with no value beyond their silver content, a camera made in Borneo, an almost worthless diamond-chip ring with molecule-thin gold plating. In the big scams you often end up with nothing except financial disaster.

Scams, professional disservices, and consumer frauds often rely upon the victim's lack of knowledge. Investing in some area you know little about is as risky as marrying somebody a half hour after meeting them. You might get lucky, but the odds against you are awesome.

Charlatans take great pains to present a false front of legitimacy and respectability to win your confidence. They adopt official-sounding or ultrarespectable-sounding names, such as "Mint Distribution Center" or "Veterans' Benefit Institute" or "International Fidelity Investments." They often produce fancy, authoritative look-alike documents that mimic official government notices. When they approach you in person, they are well-groomed, charming communicators, perhaps with fake credentials. Subtle flattery and conspiratorial friendliness are usually included in their act. Victims often describe them as "nice" and "charming."

There is almost always strong pressure to "act fast," because charlatans know they can't stand up to being investigated. (They are often in a hurry because the authorities are hot on their heels.) Often, they will also claim there is a need for secrecy, to keep their intended victim from checking them out.

Another common denominator is that swindlers claim or strongly imply there's no risk. Huge profits or wondrous personal transformations with no risks just don't happen in this world.

Sometimes fading celebrities stoop to promoting scams and semiscams because they themselves have been duped or because they need the money to maintain their lavish lifestyles. So don't buy that gap insurance or vibrating pillow or give to the Crippled Kittens Fund just because some old favorite "name" is hawking it.

Swindlers justify their actions by claiming that their victims had larceny in their hearts anyway and were willing to get something for nothing, so they were fair game. Most are also addicted to a high-flying lifestyle that they'll do anything to maintain. Whatever their justifications, they show no compassion whatsoever for their victims.

Here are some generic rules to help you steer clear of these characters:

* If any offer sounds too good to be true, you can be virtually certain that it is. These are words to live by.
* Never rush or impulse buy. Swindlers don't want to give you any time to think it over because your common sense might prevail. Plausible reasons for "acting now" will be given, such as "the deal is a closeout." But it is better to wait and lose an opportunity than to take the plunge and lose everything you have. Other opportunities always come along—nest eggs don't.
* Here are some responses to help you separate the good guys from the bad guys. One of the best is "Well, let

me talk this over with my (attorney, son, financial adviser)." Another good one is "I'll check this out with the Better Business Bureau and get back to you." Charlatans will often leave or hang up in haste, because they can't stand up to investigation. If it is a recommended professional treatment, always say you'll need a second opinion. The general idea is to let offerers know you're going to check with others about whatever they are offering or recommending.

* If an offer is in person or by phone, insist they send you written details. You'll need such details anyway to make a rational decision. Never agree to repairs on your home or car without estimates and warranties in writing. If worst comes to worst, these provide legal evidence. (Some convicted swindlers also said they feared the tough mail fraud laws.)

* Go ahead and do check out any offer or recommendation thoroughly. Call your local Area Agency on Aging or Better Business Bureau or Consumer Protection Agency or all of them. Check to be sure that any professional person is board-certified by his or her professional association and get that second opinion. Any opportunity or treatment is only as good as the people behind it.

* Investigate and comparison shop as you would with any major purchase. Check it out with more knowledgeable people—your network can be extremely valuable here. Ask lots of questions, read the fine print carefully, sleep on it. Don't be blinded by your dreams or anxieties. Very clever people are staying up late nights figuring out how to bamboozle you and me.

* Don't sign anything until you've done your investigation.

If possible, have someone in the know check over any documents or agreement before you sign.

* Use credit cards, or at least checks, never cash. There are two good reasons for this. First, with credit cards and checks there is a legal record. Second, if you see through the scheme or come to your senses in a few hours, you can cancel or stop payment.

* Never give out your credit card, Medicare, social security, telephone calling card, or bank account numbers to solicitors. Swindlers often claim they need such numbers to verify your identity as a customer or prizewinner. But give no personal information unless you initiated the transaction or you know exactly with whom you are dealing.

* The fact that an offer appears on network TV or in a respected magazine or major newspaper means *nothing*. Acceptance standards for ads are notoriously lax and virtually anyone can buy advertising. In truth the media should always print or display: "Important Notice: Let the Buyer Beware!" Even many of the regional senior newspapers I've examined are sprinkled with some very questionable ads.

* Any course of action can have unforeseen side effects or unintended consequences, so beware anyone touting "little or no risk."

* If you do get taken, please don't be too embarrassed to report it to the police, your local attorney general, the Better Business Bureau, Area Agency on Aging, and any relevant professional association—as widely as possible. Also report anything suspicious, even if you don't fall for it. You might help save many others from being hurt.

#41

Telemarketing Frauds

Seniors seem to be the special phone targets of investment, home repair, vacation, social security, and Medicare schemers, but just about every other imaginable scam is tried on us too. My dinnertime is interrupted at least twice a week by these characters.

When you hear the word "Congratulations!" from a computer-generated voice or stranger over your phone, you can just hang up. Or if there's a 900 number you have to call, you pay by the minute and you can be virtually certain it is not legitimate. Legitimate offers do occasionally come in cold over your phone, for instance, from companies or professionals you have been dealing with. But even here, insist they send you something in writing so you can examine it in detail at your leisure and run some checks on its authenticity. A halfway reliable guideline is that calls you initiate tend to be safer than incoming calls to you.

That "free trip to the Bahamas" is too good to be true. The home repair company that calls might or might not be on the up and up, but you certainly want to check out their track record. Even the man with the nice phone voice who is collecting for the firemen's fund needs a verification check. And the "Merry Friend Dating Service" could be any sort of scam. When I've asked around, I've found many older people who have been hoodwinked at least for small sums by telemarketing solicitors, but I've found less than a handful who got anything worthwhile.

Never give out your credit card number over the phone to unknown solicitors. Many will come up with ingenious schemes to get your account numbers, then charge them up to the limit, often in cahoots with dishonest store employees. One common ploy is to claim they need your card or bank account number to verify your identity as a prizewinner. Be immediately wary of any unknown person probing for any personal information about you. Crooks have posed as federal bank examiners and even IRS agents to get such information for their own nasty purposes. (Legitimate government agencies contact you by mail.)

Having an unlisted number is no protection from telemarketing scams. Modern "boiler rooms" are often set up where banks of computers dial numbers randomly until someone answers. Also, if you've ever responded before to these schemes, your name is probably now on "sucker lists" that dishonest outfits sell back and forth among themselves. Besides your name, these lists usually have your age, marital status, shopping habits, hobbies, and sometimes employment and medical data.

These outfits peddle everything from time-share vacation homes to insurance to rare coin investments to vitamins to love matches—all bogus. They are almost impossible to curb because by the time the authorities find out about them and start to take action, they've usually already swindled scores or hundreds of people and moved on. So you must be your own guardian.

Listen if you want to, but know that it's virtually certain there's a sharpie on the other end of the line. The best advice is to just hang up. If you do need some service, there are no doubt as good or better deals around.

#42

Mail Fraud

Mrs. Mary Mark has won one of the following prizes" arrives in the mail, in an official-looking envelope marked "Postmaster: Priority Mail." All you need do to claim your prize is send $9.95 for shipping and handling or attend this meeting at a local posh hotel to learn about a wonderful retirement community. In truth the prize is a worthless trinket made by sweatshop workers in a Third World country, and the retirement community is an untouched, dusty southwestern wasteland.

Because of stiff mail fraud penalties, swindlers who use the mails strive to be especially clever in their smoke-and-mirrors wordings. After all, they can claim, the person *did* get a prize (worth twenty cents) and the person *can* buy a lot (highly overpriced) where there might be a retirement community built *someday*. What charlatans like about the mails is that they can cheaply reach high numbers of people, and if even a tiny fraction of recipients tumbles for their tricks, they become rich.

Again, there are legitimate offers and product ads that arrive through the mail, such a catalogs and grocery store ads. Legitimate firms have usually been around for a while, offer (somewhat) honest products with sufficient information so you can comparison shop, have toll-free numbers so you can get questions answered, and can survive a call to the Better Business Bureau. They want your money, too, and their product claims almost certainly stretch the truth. And even many of our most prestigious name-brand companies keep getting caught at bending the laws out of shape. But they're not dedicated crooks. In addition to observing the generic scam-thwarting guidelines already outlined, here are some good tactics for avoiding the true swindles.

- Read through the piece of mail, then set it aside, perhaps for a day or two. Then do a fresh reading, looking for the catches. You'll find that you often see through the smokescreen, or you'll have come up with enough doubts to just throw it away.
- Don't merely read the offer; study it. If there's fine print, study that closely, too. (You can get a pocket magnifying glass at any dime store; I carry one with me always.)
- If the offer concerns some topic you know little about, ask someone in your network who knows more. This isn't foolproof, but it will help you eliminate the shoddiest come-ons. For example, anyone who knows much about real estate can warn you that undeveloped land is usually a terrible investment. In most cases, you're better off not even getting into an area with which you haven't been previously acquainted—even though the offer is dazzling.
- Many people have adopted a strict fail-safe tactic. Once they've sorted their incoming mail, they simply throw away all such unsolicited offers without even reading them.

#43

Dodging Street Scams

There's a small crowd around the fellow with an open truck or car trunk, and some kind of transactions are taking place. Or someone approaches you with a strange story about finding money. Or you are out working in your yard and a guy stops by in a repair vehicle, says his crew is working in the neighborhood and can clean your gutters, weatherproof your house, or seal your driveway for a fraction of the ordinary cost with their leftover materials.

When you are outside or on the street, if you are approached by anyone with any sort of money-making deal or hard luck story or offer of "special merchandise," you can be absolutely, positively certain you have been marked and it's a scam. No exceptions. If you are approached with a hard luck story, direct the person to a church or social agency. (Such "strays" too often turn out to be wolves.) Any fantastic bargain is either stolen or a fake. (You break the law by buying stolen goods.)

If anyone stops you with a "special offer," keep walking. Street swindlers often work in teams, so don't be surprised if someone else "innocently" shows up to play their part in the staged encounter. The best advice in any such situation is, walk on by.

The rule by which to protect yourself is simple and inflexible: Never make a deal on the street.

#44

Seeing Through False Advertising and Marketing

Loans While You Wait." "Doctor-approved Hair Restoration." "Earn $$$ Working at Home." "Invest in Gold." "Free Hearing Tests." "Giant Going Out of Business Sale." "No More Arthritis Pain." All newspaper, TV, and magazine ads are carefully crafted to entice you to buy some product or service. "Truth in advertising" is almost a contradiction in terms, whether the source is legitimate or not. So all ads and commercials should be examined with a cool, suspicious head.

All ads make strong claims and use provocative, emotional images to get you to be a consumer—and even the government can get into the act. (During a recent economic downturn, both public officials and private economists scolded the nation's debt-ridden consumers for not spending more.) So even legitimate companies and government officials have a rapacious attitude toward us consumers. Legitimate ads are seductive, but the swindler is a financial rapist.

Advertisements do sometimes serve a useful purpose. They inform us of new products and services that might improve our lives. But we need to distinguish between objective claims, persuasive hype, and outright criminal lies.

If you don't know the merchandise, know the merchant. If you plan to buy goods or services you are unfamiliar with, your best first bet is to *deal only with established, reputable firms.* This is no guarantee at all, but it will probably save you from the worst ripoffs.

Check it out remains the guiding principle. Reputable ads will deliver something for something, even if the "something" you get isn't everything you hoped and dreamed it would be. If you tumble for fraudulent ads you get virtually nothing. For instance, a reputable store will give you an automatic washer in exchange for several hundred dollars—and it does wash the clothes. A "solar-energy dryer" from a fly-by-night outfit takes your large check and sends you fifty cents worth of clothespins (this is an actual case). Legitimate firms also have warranties and return policies that protect you, at least to some extent.

There are two levels of checking it out, and each is important. First, is the outfit an outright scam? If you're shopping for something you are familiar with, like grocery specials where you know the stores, this first level isn't necessary. But there are faddish items and even fad surgeries, so you might want to check out the real story on items or services offered even from legitimate outfits. Are air purifiers or a facelift really a worthwhile investment? We've all seen so many times how today's craze can so easily become tomorrow's worthless gizmo or professional scandal.

Every human being gets anxious sometimes about personal circumstances. As seniors, we may have special uneasiness about our finances or our health. This is when we are most likely to fall for a loan or investment or job opportunity or miracle cure swindles. So this is precisely the time we need to be most careful in checking out advertisements that come our way.

Don't impulse buy. Even if the item or service proves to be legitimate, do you need it? Sleep on it before going ahead. Selling people things they don't really need or want—unnecessary goods and services—is a subtle scam too widely practiced by even reputable firms.

The second level of checking it out involves comparing prices and quality. Why pay double just for a label? Virtually every item or service varies greatly in price and quality, even hospital costs. Malls are almost always more expensive than discount and outlet stores, and you don't need a $400-an-hour "name" lawyer to file a routine paper or an oral surgeon to fill a tooth. *Consumer Reports* and the various other consumer guides are especially worthwhile. Also, ask around in your network: it can be a wonderful source of pooled experience and wisdom for avoiding unnecessary expense.

Keep in mind that many companies and professionals who advertise are more concerned about their own profits than they are with you. Most major companies have been nailed for fraud and misleading advertising more than once. And understaffed regulatory agencies only catch a few of the worst offenses. So, we're left with that most ancient advice to the consumer: Let the buyer beware!

#45

Retirement and Financial Ripoffs

Double Your Nest Egg: High Yields, No Risk." "Come Join Us in Beautiful Alligator Acres." In the United States, people over sixty-five make up only one-eighth of the population, yet they account for one-third of all the major financial fraud victims, and the figures are similar in most other modern countries. There is a simple reason for these facts: Older people have the lion's share of accumulated resources and the swindlers (and legitimate promoters) know it. (What resources you and I have might seem very modest to us, but they make the jackals hungry.)

Crooks, hucksters, and legitimate promoters target pitches toward people around retirement age. They know there are often lump-sum pension settlements, IRA turnovers, dreams of relocating, travel plans, and insurance concerns, and they want a piece of the action. This is also the time when people are setting up trusts and wills, readjusting their investment nest eggs, deciding what to do with the equity in their homes, and so on. Even the legitimate promoters want to steer you their way, into their programs, because they can often collect commissions in addition to and far above what they charge you.

The ins and outs of retirement and financial planning go well beyond the scope of this book, but crime-wise there are some pointers to keep firmly in mind.

"If you want good service, serve yourself," says the old Spanish proverb. These decisions involve large sums and major life courses, so take your time, find out as much as you can, and call your own shots. For instance, consider enrolling in a financial planning course at your local community college. Read up on retirement and investment options at your library.

Verify the credentials and track record of anyone you deal with—financial planners, real estate agents, lawyers, insurance salespeople, investment brokers. The laws are leaky in many of these areas, so be your own private investigator. Good credentials are still no guarantee that professionals will do their best for you, but this research will help weed out the worst.

Ask for recommendations from your network. This is no absolute guarantee either, but it is far safer than selecting from the Yellow Pages or because of glitzy promotional materials. Service people you approach tend to be a better bet than such persons who solicit you.

It can be tempting just to go for the first likely-seeming opportunity in a retirement location or financial investment and be done with it. This is usually a big mistake. Take your time, do some homework, don't agree to any place or plan sight unseen, and check out alternatives. For instance, settling in a small town might give you everything you'd find in a highly promoted retirement community at half the price. And you can park your money in an insured savings account or reliable low-risk mutual fund (with no front-end or exit fees) while you really explore the alternatives. Also, your own hard-won common sense can be at least as reliable as the technical showiness of experts, so don't be stampeded or overawed by them. Remember how many times the "experts" have been dead wrong about everything in recent years.

You can get a great deal of help on major retirement and finance questions free or at little cost, so don't just agree to pay large up-front adviser fees. Check with your local aging agency, the personnel department where you work, senior legal and tax aid services, your network, a local librarian, and so on. You may save thousands of dollars. Check at least three different sources if you plan on refinancing your home, for example; fees vary greatly.

Always inquire about the fees, any additional monthly or yearly costs, guarantees, and refunds when exploring a senior housing complex, financial plan, or care center. And get it in writing. Large fees tend to equal scam.

Nowadays, every major housing, legal, or financial move is bedeviled with documents; these should always be approached with extreme wariness. *In most cases, the clauses are there to protect someone else, not you!* And far too often, a clause buried on the back pages or in the fine print can turn out to be a disaster. Once you sign, you can be stuck.

If you sometimes have trouble making sense out of contracts and legal documents, join the club. Research has shown that people of all ages and educational levels have trouble comprehending such forms. Often the fine print is hard for anyone, including experts with 20/20 vision, to read, let alone grasp. (It took me a day and a half, a calculator, and several phone calls to make sense out of a two-page form from a midwestern state government.)

Never sign a document until you fully understand what it says. (Even a contract signed with a proven crook is often binding.) Read over the document several times, just as you might do with a difficult school lesson. I have made this an inflexible practice for decades and it has served me handsomely. If someone's in a hurry for me to sign, that's their problem.

For anything more than a minor transaction, it is wise to have someone who is on your side go over the forms. You can probably pay a real estate or paralegal acquaintance from your network a few dollars to check it all over. Perhaps there is even someone in your network or at the local senior center who is knowledgeable in the area. For a major transaction, a hundred dollars would be money well spent.

After you've made any large deal, *continue to monitor how it is progressing.* Never just assume that everything is now automatically taken care of, or that others will faithfully perform their end of the bargain. Check over all subsequent statements and documents carefully. As one example, consumer groups have found that adjustable rate mortgages are miscalculated almost half the time, and that the errors are usually overcharges.

Remember, it's better to pass up a good deal than gamble on a questionable one.

#46

Home Repair Frauds

We've been working in your neighborhood and we have some leftover materials; we can do it cheap." These charlatans appeal to our love of a bargain, a deal where we can save a bundle on some home repair we've been putting off. Or a "utility inspector" stops by, takes our furnace apart, claims it has a dangerous fault, but tells us conspiratorially he has a brother who can do the repairs cut rate. Or we find a loose roof tile, call a "reputable" company from the Yellow Pages and they inform us we need an entire new roof. In each of these three scenarios, we are teetering on the verge of being taken.

With the workers, we should ask, "What neighbors?" and let the fellow know we're going to check out his story. We should call the utility company and ask if the "inspector" is for real, then call the police if he is not. And we can ask an experienced handyman from our network if we will be fine (and much richer) just having the roof tile replaced. (These are all actual cases.)

- Never let an unsolicited stranger talk you into believing your home needs some repair. Even if it does, you'll want to check out the repair person thoroughly and comparison shop. I've found that you can almost always get a job done well for half or less the price of some of the estimates.

• Never sign any repair contract without checking out the wording and the workers. Some of these contracts have liens or binding clauses in the fine print that can make you liable even to a swindler. Also, any materials and workmanship warranties are no better than the company offering them.

• Unless you're dealing with a trusted handyman, ensure that the repair company is properly licensed. Your local senior center, municipal office, or attorney general's office can help you do this.

• If someone comes to your door, never purchase their services without thoroughly checking them out.

• Always demand a written estimate on any repair work. Never pay in cash. Never pay more than a down payment for materials until the job is complete. And don't accept any significant overruns of the estimate.

• When you get estimates, don't be deceived by amazingly low bids. You're too likely to get amazingly poor workmanship and inferior materials. In one case, for example, all "special waterproof paint" washed off during the first rain.

• Never pay all of a repair bill if there are still "just a few things to finish up." Insist that the job be completely finished and inspect it closely before paying everything. Twice I've failed to do this, to my sorrow.

• With your network, develop a pool of reliable, reasonably priced handymen, plumbers, electricians, roofers, and so on. This one step can save you a fortune. Satisfactory service, spread by word of mouth, is your best guide.

#47

Getting Honest Professional Service

As seniors, we often need and want many kinds of services from professionals. So how do we find a good doctor, dentist, financial adviser, car mechanic, real estate agent, or other professional who will serve our needs and not take advantage of the fact that we aren't an expert in that area? Most professionals are both honest and competent, but some are neither.

The fraudulent pro has two things going for him or her: (1) our lack of knowledge and (2) the very human habit of taking advice from someone who appears to be in the know (after all, this is why we're seeking an expert).

Most of us are in no position to judge the niceties of CD versus municipal bond nest-egg investments, decide on the necessity of a hip joint replacement, or say whether we need a new dental bridge. We sometimes have to rely on experts, but we aren't helpless.

Take the trouble to verify the professional's authenticity and reputation. Most professions now have associations that certify members and hold them to at least some minimum level of competence and ethical standards. A disturbing number of bogus "pros" will simply lie to you about their authenticity, so run your own check.

Especially if a major expenditure or service is involved, indicate to the professional that you want to check out the recommendation with others. If you are strongly discouraged from doing so, you can almost be certain the alleged pro has something to hide, so go elsewhere.

Ask a professional you do trust and have worked with for referrals to pros in other fields they might know of. Your dentist might help you find a nontoxic family doctor or vice versa. This is no guarantee, but it's far better than nothing. So are recommendations from folks you respect in your network.

If you feel uneasy about a professional when first visiting him or her, listen to your gut feelings and go elsewhere. If nothing else, the chemistry for a good professional-client relationship won't be there.

Be very wary of any professional who discourages you from asking questions. Part of their job is to explain the situation to the point where you understand what's up and what your options are. Always keep in mind that their assessments are only judgment calls, not gospel truths, and any final decision must be up to you. Professionals sometimes get arrogant, but remember, they're working for you.

Inquire about fees up front so you don't have any nasty surprises. Get itemized statements, audit them before paying, and keep copies. Don't hesitate to challenge any billing item; I've often found that the professional will make a settlement to avoid further hassles.

Find out about the subject—osteoporosis, tooth implants, incontinence, term insurance, living trusts, car engines, whatever. The more you know, the less vulnerable you will be. People sometimes balk at this step (and professionals sometimes discourage them), but getting some familiarity with a subject is usually easier than you might think. Your local reference librarian is your best ally in this, and the publications of consumer advocate groups shouldn't be overlooked.

Unless it is an emergency and you have no choice, never select a professional cold out of the Yellow Pages. Virtually any other selection scheme is better.

If you run afoul of a bogus professional or know about a case, get the data out as widely as possible. Turn them in. Notify their professional association, your state attorney general, the Better Business Bureau, and the local senior center. If you've been abused or bilked financially, consider seeing a lawyer.

Unnecessary services are the major risk in working with any professional or tradesperson and must be watched out for. All such people make their living selling their services, so it should come as no surprise that they tend to promote and recommend them. Unnecessary services comprise the majority of complaints filed. A dentist unnecessarily crowns all our teeth; a mechanic overrepairs our car; an insurance company sells us expensive unneeded gap insurance; a nutritionist sells us esoteric herbs from the Himalayas when more fruits and veggies and a multimineral tab would do the trick; a doctor recommends elective major surgery when a chiropractor could align our back or neck and show us how to relax for a tiny fraction of the cost, pain, and risk. Those who peddle such services may not be charlatans, but they are interested in themselves and their own financial bottom lines. The preceding pointers will help you stay out of their clutches.

#48

Medical Frauds

During the last century incredible strides have been made in health care, sanitation, and nutrition, and we all benefit from these advances. Yet the consumer must keep a wary eye out for medical quacks on the one hand and abuses by the legitimate health care industry on the other. Over one-eighth of all the money spent in America goes for some sort of health care, and there's fierce competition for these megadollars, so the wolves are out in force.

There are endless controversies now raging in the health care field—biological versus emotional risk factors, nutrition versus drug therapy, exercise and lifestyle changes versus elective surgeries—and no one yet has all the answers.

Into this confused arena comes the medical charlatan, who offers the anxious and desperate "cures" that are at best worthless and at worst deadly. They offer machines with flashing lights to energize body organs, magnetic bracelets to reverse arthritis, isometric facelift devices, secret rejuvenation formulas from some hidden valley tribe, and paper prayer rugs to resolve all your problems at one kneeling. Diet scams abound and the plans are often more dangerous than being overweight. There are even witches who will cast any spell for you—health, love, or vengeance—just send your money.

The standard advice is always to check with your doctor. Yet this may not be a safe course either. Studies have shown there is a high rate of unnecessary surgeries. For example, Dr. Joseph Giordan, President Reagan's lifesaver, has asserted that there are far too many heart bypass surgeries and vascular diagnostic procedures being done, simply because Medicare pays for them. Also, the doctor's wife or receptionist may know more about nutrition, emotional healing, and exercise than he does.

The whole health care field is presently going through tremendous upheavals and a worldwide cost-and-delivery crisis. There's a steady march of tremendous medical breakthroughs, yet medical bills are the cause of half the personal bankruptcies in the United States. We all have to navigate between the doctors who are overeager to push surgeries and prescriptions and the health care quacks. Members of either camp may swindle and even kill us. But we can take some steps to enhance the likelihood of getting the best care and avoiding the worst.

Always focus on decent nutrition and moderate exercise, which are under your direct control and have proven so important in maintaining health and quality of life at any age. This will help keep both the doctors and the quacks away.

It's worthwhile to become knowledgeable about health issues. Presently, *Prevention* magazine and Rodale Press books are some of the best sources of information. If you have a particular condition, such as angina or hearing problems, learn all you can about it. Dig into the subject at your library, ask tons of questions, don't take anyone's claims on faith, consult sources with different viewpoints. Be a savvy consumer, as you would in any other area. Be wary of anyone who discourages you from doing this.

Check any health care professional's credentials and record. You can call the doctor certification line at (800)776-2378 to verify that a doctor has been certified by the American Board of Medical Specialties. (In a survey by the prestigious *New England Journal of Medicine*, one out of eight M.D. "specialists" listed in the Yellow Pages were actually not board-certified.)

If it isn't an emergency and a physician recommends surgery or other invasive treatments, ask lots of questions before deciding. The U.S. Department of Health and Human Services and consumer advocate groups recommend asking the following questions: What is wrong with me? What is the planned operation or treatment? What are the probable benefits? What are the risks and in what percent of cases do they occur? What will happen if I don't have the surgery or treatment? How long does recovery take and are there residual side effects? What nonsurgical alternatives are there to try first? What is the cost—including all postoperative expenses?

Second (or more) opinions should be a way of life; both governmental health agencies and insurance companies recommend and sometimes demand them. (In one out of four cases, second opinions do not confirm the original recommendations.) It is important to get an independent second opinion, not from someone on the same medical team as your doctor. You can also go outside traditional medicine for second opinions, for instance, to a licensed nutritionist, chiropractor, or physician who is a member of the American

Holistic Medical Association. Nutritionists have often handled adult-onset diabetes through nutrition alone, and chiropractors have saved some people from having to have back or neck surgery.

Find out if your doctor is an investment partner in any medical facility he or she refers you to. In a Florida study patients of such doctors were alleged to have received 45 percent more lab tests than other patients. Your doctor may be totally ethical about this situation, but it is an inherent conflict of interest.

Health care advertisements and direct solicitations are a minefield of false claims and outright scams. "Free examination" offers are too often come-ons for unnecessary services or schemes for bilking Medicare. Most miracle weight-loss or anti-aging products are just reincarnations of the old snake-oil game. Much cosmetic surgery is questionable and risky. And you can lease a home emergency response system from a reputable hospital or have the feature tied in to your home security alarm system for one-fifth the cost of some highly touted commercial systems.

The over-the-counter drug and cosmetic industry is ridden with small scams. Product claims are sometimes sheer fantasy. But the most common ripoffs are expensive name-brand items, which are usually no better by chemical analysis than generic discount equivalents. You can save a bundle over time by comparison shopping and buying discount store equivalents for pain relievers, allergy medicines, and so on. Always ask your doctor for generic drug prescriptions. (The U.S. Senate Committee on Aging claims that prices for drugs used by seniors have skyrocketed in recent years, without reason.)

Examine all health care billings closely and suspiciously.

If you are still recuperating and not up to this, have it done by a family or network member. The "errors" even from highly respected institutions have often been outrageous. Hospitals and clinics sometimes even charge you for making out your bill.

Make your own decisions—it's your body, your health, and your life. And have hope. I know personally of a great many seniors who have recovered from major medical conditions.

#49

Charitable and Religious Donations

There are thousands of organizations working hard to help those in need and to make our world a better place. Without their efforts, our planet would be far more dismal. And in an outpouring of generosity, many seniors support such organizations with their money and willing hands.

It should come as no surprise that swindlers get into the act by creating bogus look-alike relief funds, foundations, and charitable causes. The names might sound lofty, there might be inspiring pleas, the appeals might be emotional, and the cause righteous. But in many cases, little or none of the aid ever reaches any needy recipients. Scandal after scandal has also recently come to light where cult and religious leaders have siphoned off congregation funds for their own personal enrichment. Too often, their overseas orphanages or missionary crusades have turned out to be hoaxes.

The single burning question is, what percent of the money or goods goes directly to the cause? You are fairly safe with well-established charities such as the United Way, yet even here there have been some recent scandals. The two most common abuses are sound-alike charities, such as the Unified Way or the National Cancer Relief Fund, and "designer" charities that dovetail with current events, such as the Third World Relief Fund or the Persian Gulf Veterans Assistance Foundation. If there's a disaster, such as the L.A. riots or widespread hurricane havoc, charlatans rush in with often widely advertised bogus "relief funds." If you want to contribute, your best bet is to stick with the Red Cross. Sometimes the scam artists stay within the letter of the law by actually donating a small portion of their take to the purported cause; sometimes the swindlers just take it all and disappear.

A special problem exists with religious organizations because of the laws that shield them from the same inspection to which other groups are subject. Cults and some televangelists have often hidden behind these shielding constitutional laws, so choose where you tithe with care.

Never donate to an organization, no matter how well promoted or how heart-tugging the appeal, without checking out its reputation—specifically, how much goes to recipients and how much to overhead and salaries. A good rule of thumb is that fund-raising expenses and salaries shouldn't run more than 25 percent.

In the United States, the Better Business Bureau's Philanthropic Advisory Service, 400 Wilshire Blvd., Arlington, VA 22203, will send you free reports on most national charities if you enclose a self-addressed stamped business envelope.

Many think tanks and foundations, despite their lofty names, are essentially front groups for very partisan political positions or the special interests of commercial industries. So you'll want to examine their literature and positions to see how they match your own before giving them your financial or volunteer support.

#50

Curbing Corporate Crimes

It was only a few years ago that most people didn't take white collar and corporation crimes very seriously. The FBI didn't even gather statistics on them. All that has now changed because we've seen scandal after scandal at the corporate level and we've all inherited the widespread devastation resulting. Most of our major corporations have been indicted or are under investigation for serious criminal malpractice. Such "trickle-down" crimes as the savings and loan scandals have put even our grandchildren in hock.

Although most people are more fearful of street crimes, corporate crimes are actually far more costly and dangerous to the average person. The chance that we'll all be defrauded this year by such crimes is 100 percent. Those with far-reaching power in a society can commit more far-reaching crimes, with a far greater number of victims.

Corporate crimes don't usually involve the personal shocks of violent street crimes, but are you shocked by your tax bills or the unexpected layoff of a friend? "Bottom-line fever" is the prime motivating factor behind these crimes. According to corporate crime researcher Stuart Hills, this fever for profit has produced a business atmosphere where the overwhelming drive is for success and recognition, a ruthless quest for expansion and short-term profits, strong pressures to produce through any means, distance from any consequences of one's actions, and "ethical numbness."

The extent of corporate crime is both astounding and dismaying. Russell Mokhiber, a widely recognized expert, in his book *Corporate Crime and Violence* documents how such crimes cost several hundred billion dollars annually, cause thousands of deaths and injuries, are environmentally corrosive, and impoverish our way of life. Few of the guilty executives are ever arrested; most cases are settled in civil hearings. Even if arrested and convicted, few of the guilty ever spend even a single day in jail. Those who work in federal and state regulatory agencies are usually dedicated, but they are hampered by evaporating budgets, political pressure to "cool it," and lack of real teeth in their regulations.

But times are changing. Public outrage over white collar crime, such as the savings and loan and defense contract scandals, is increasing. State and local attorneys general are now beginning to prosecute corporate misbehavior aggressively. Many private consumer protection groups have also sprung up to provide consumer information, publicize infractions, and initiate legal actions. People often feel helpless in the face of corporate crimes, but we are not helpless. Steps can be taken.

Use consumer-oriented publications, such as *Consumer Reports*, when contemplating purchases. These contain money-saving tips and objective evaluations of major and minor items. Your local library will probably have these. There are also consumer information books, such as Ralph

Nader's *The Frugal Shopper*. Using such sources saves you money, rewards honest businesses, and takes business away from the shabby ones.

Report instances or suspected instances of consumer fraud, workplace negligence, illegal toxic dumping, or other corporate crimes to your local and state attorney general. The phone number and address will be in the government section of your telephone directory, or ask your operator for assistance. (The police are not equipped to deal with most forms of corporate crime unless direct personal or property harm is involved.)

An easy further step is to join such consumer support and industry watchdog groups as Common Cause and the Sierra Club. The AARP and the AAA also perform consumer advocate functions, and there are similar groups in other countries. Membership fees for such groups are modest and each additional member increases their clout. They also have many volunteer activities for those who want to be more actively involved.

If the world is ever to be safe, corporations and their executives will need to be held accountable for their actions. General Douglas MacArthur used to say, "There is no security on this earth; there is only opportunity." Most of us know this and are willing to take our chances in the game of life. But swindlers cheat us by rigging the game so that we can only lose. If you follow the guidelines in this chapter, however, you are almost certain to thwart them.

#51

How to Complain Effectively

If you get taken by a con artist the chances of recovering your money are not very good, although the quicker you report the incident to the authorities, the better your odds.

If you have received unsatisfactory service from a company or a professional, your chance of getting the matter handled is far better. In these uncertain economic times, companies and professionals have become more sensitive to consumer complaints because their reputations are so important for business. They are also growing more leery of local, state, and federal regulatory agencies. A bad reputation can be very bad for business, which is sometimes the most effective weapon a complainant has.

Don't hesitate to complain about unsatisfactory goods, services, or treatment by employees. *Perseverance* is your most effective strategy. As the saying goes, "The squeaky wheel gets the grease." Ask for and write down the names and positions of those you deal with in both private and public organizations. If you get no satisfaction, kick the problem upstairs to more senior personnel.

A polite but firm verbal complaint is the first step. Talk

with the person who was directly involved in delivering the goods or services. Often this will succeed because the company or professional wants to save further hassles and prevent more formal complaints. But you may only be met with excuses and justifications (sometimes because of the false myths about aging outlined in entry #1). Keep a written record of the names, details, and dates of your verbal attempt.

If you get no results from your informal complaint, put it in writing. State the problem clearly and what you want as a fair settlement. Include copies of all pertinent receipts, contracts, documents, and erroneous billings. Never send original documents. State how you've tried to handle the situation informally and the details of what happened. The letter should be brief, clear, and polite, but firm. And be sure to keep copies. If it's a company, send the letter to "Customer Service," if a professional, directly to him or her.

If you don't get any reply within ten days or so or if you get the runaround, write another letter, this time to the president of the company or head of the professional group. State what you've done so far and firmly ask that the matter be settled. From this point on you should probably send registered letters and spend the small cost to get back delivery receipts.

If still no settlement is offered, write again stating that if your complaint is not handled you will feel forced to take further action, such as informing the Better Business Bureau, the state attorney general, any relevant professional association or watchdog regulatory agency. If you have grounds for legal action, state your intention to pursue them if necessary. This sequence of actions lets the other party know that

(1) you aren't just going to go away and (2) they have a potentially troublesome situation on their hands.

If none of this has worked, "go for it." Check to see if you have a worthwhile legal case with an attorney, but be wary of getting caught up in a web of legal fees. You might consider small claims court as an alternative. Someone at the local aging agency or legal aid might be able to help you at this point. Whatever else you do, inform all the agencies you had threatened to. Also tell your friends and the people in your network so they'll be forewarned against similar consumer fraud.

#52

Claiming Your Share

You may be robbing yourself.

Surveys by the AARP and various consumer groups have shown that a great many seniors do not take advantage of the many discounts, benefits, and compensations they have coming. The main reason is that they don't know about such benefits. Another reason is that they "don't feel right" about taking them. But all of us who have raised kids or maintained a home or held down a job or all of the above for decades certainly have paid our dues. Yet half of all older people eligible for government financial and medical assistance don't receive it. And many seniors pay full rates for transportation, meals, travel, and even overpay taxes, resulting in needless expenses and benefits not taken.

In his field research, Robert Veninga found that claiming one's share of available resources and benefits was very often the secret of retiring successfully on a modest income. He found that it took a bit of digging and doing, but the payoffs were handsome—hundreds, even thousands of dollars a year in reduced expenses. Some seniors even make a game out of this, striving never to pay full price for anything.

A good technique is to build up a file of these discounts and benefits just as a cook builds a file of recipes. For starters, there are senior discounts on meals, hotels, buses, trains, planes, some cab companies, movies, parks, and recreation. There are Meals on Wheels and Dial-A-Ride programs and inexpensive meals at senior centers. Many stores have a designated day when seniors get a discount on all purchases. Your local library or senior center probably has a free tax-preparation service. And there are many local and state and federal assistance programs that all seniors are eligible for. Very often you need to ask about these services; in most cases you are not automatically notified of them.

One effective strategy that many senior networks and centers have come up with is to pool their information about benefits and services. Sometimes they photocopy listed information and use bulletin boards to spread the word. One California senior center has adopted the motto: "We Never Pay Full Price!"

Two very useful books to help you claim your fair share are John Howells's *Retirement on a Shoestring* and Amy and Armond Budish's *Golden Opportunities*.

Developing a Crime-free Lifestyle

In crime avoidance, solid research has shown that there are lifestyle factors that are as important as locking up and staying near other people. How we conduct our lives has a surprisingly strong influence on how crime-free we stay. There is no intention to preach morals here or tell you how to live your life. But you do need to know the facts about the risks, then steer your own course. Many seniors have also found this data very useful in dealing with others, choosing companions, and handling friends and relatives who are victim-prone.

#53

Victim Proneness

Some people go through their whole lives without having a serious brush with crime, while others are repeatedly victimized. When crime researchers realized this fact they began scrambling to search out the differences between the crime-free and crime-prone groups. They found a number of things that contributed directly to victim proneness. What follows are good clues about what not to do.

Obvious negligence. Criminals observe such negligence and mark the person or property as an easy target. Even criminologists and off-duty police officers have been known to engage in negligent habits, such as casually walking down "mean streets" alone, keeping a loaded gun in plain sight around the house, or falling for fast-talking swindlers. Most of the earlier entries in this book provide antidotes to such negligent habits, but the victimization of even crime professionals shows that *it isn't what you know, it's what you do.*

Persisting in crime-prone habits even after a victimization incident. Criminologist John Conklin found that many armed robbery victims in the Boston area continued to go out alone and be in isolated situations. It is crucial to learn from any direct or indirect crime experience and take steps to change any habits or factors that might have contributed to it.

Provocation. Seniors can put themselves at greater risk by abrasive interpersonal habits and by participating in risk-filled situations. Having a chip on one's shoulder or needlessly antagonizing others is hazardous. Provocation means that in some manner the victim had a hand in precipitating the crime.

Frequent intoxication. Police investigators continue to be amazed at how often liquor is involved in crimes in which seniors are either victims or perpetrators—family violence, muggings, assaults, elder abuse, and homicides. Tipsy revelers, for instance, are a criminal's delight, and people often seriously injure their spouses in inebriated anger. Also, the House Select Committee on Aging found that half of all nursing home residents have alcohol-related problems. (With young people, both drugs and alcohol greatly increase all crime risks.)

Illegal activities. Veteran police officers can cite numerous cases of older people who eventually came to grief because they regularly flirted with the wild side of life. Criminals expect—rightly so—that such victims will not report what's done to them or testify in court, because the victims were also breaking the law and would at least risk disgrace. People who are looking to score illicit goods or services should know that there are those in the shadows who are planning to score on them. Those who provide such illegal goods and services—gambling, prostitution, shady deals, and so on—are often "nice" to their marks, but this should never be mistaken for friendship; marks are targets for exploitation. And somewhere inside every criminal network lurk some really ugly characters.

Ignoring intuitions. Time and time again, victims say they ignored the warning signs or inner promptings or uneasy feelings that they had. But they went ahead anyway and ran afoul of crime. Seniors shouldn't ignore these hunches even when they seem entirely unfounded. If they turn out wrong, and there was no danger, probably nothing is lost. If the hunch is right, but ignored, the cost can be high.

Innocence. Both street criminals and swindlers feed off people's innocence. This is one reason crime rates are so high among the young. No matter how old we are, we're all innocent about so many things outside our own bailiwick. Crime proneness arises when we proceed anyway without really knowing enough about what we're doing. Venturing into unfamiliar territory, whether downtown districts or investment plans, without doing some inquiring is a gamble. The district might have crime rates twenty times the citywide average and the investment plan might already be a national scandal. Don't go for it until you know.

Many people have some aspects of a victim-prone lifestyle, yet they've never come to grief. But because of their own risky habits, the odds may one day run against them.

If you are personally involved as a friend, romantic partner, or relative of victim-prone people, do something about it. Their habits are likely to put you more at risk, too. It's hard enough to reform oneself, let alone somebody else, but it's wise to communicate your own concerns to them. Also, consider cutting back on aspects of the relationship that put you at risk. And keep up your own precautions.

#54

Handling Dangerous Emotions

When you feel emotionally upset or dog tired or depressed or mad at the world, you are more vulnerable to being a crime victim. There's a tendency for distraught or weary people to be more careless and reckless than usual. All of us have our mood swings, but we need to reduce the crime risks they carry. People in a bad mood are

- less alert to their surroundings
- less likely to take that extra security step
- more likely to take "what the hell" stupid chances
- more likely to drink to excess
- more likely to provoke others

You can see how each of these increases victim proneness. So what do you do instead of sulking or giving the dog a whack? The aim is to get through the rotten feelings without causing harm to anyone, including yourself.

Don't go out alone when feeling down or upset if you can possibly avoid it. Going out may be something you need or want to do, but strive to do it with a supportive companion.

If you must go out by yourself, realize that you are at greater risk so be extra careful and methodical in your actions.

One alternative is to stay home and use the personal tricks you've developed over the years to cool yourself down and revitalize yourself. Take a long bath, do some physical activity, escape into a novel or sitcom, take a nap, punch a pillow, whatever.

Another good alternative is to tell a friend who is a good listener and doesn't interrupt with streams of advice. In a series of international studies, researcher Michael Argyle documented the fact that just getting an upset off your chest to a good listener can cut its force in half. If the upsets persist or rest on a chronic problem, consider joining a self-help support group such as the Older Women's League (OWL).

If you become upset or bone weary while you are out, keep enough presence of mind to maintain your security habits and get home safely.

#55

Avoiding Romantic Mishaps

Many older people become involved in romantic ventures of various sorts. Some even report that love is sweeter the second (or fifth) time around. Affairs of the heart are always something of a gamble, yet they can also cost more than just heartache. They may lead to more entanglements than you bargained for and they entail some crime risks.

Date rape is quite rare among seniors, but seduction with dishonorable intentions is not so uncommon and both sexes are at some risk. Lonely people (of any age) are vulnerable and both male and female swindlers will sometimes use their charms to coax seniors into an involvement, then defraud them. Con artists sometimes deliberately pose as the heroes of romance novels or the women of older men's dreams, sweeping the victims off their feet with charm, fervor, and attentiveness, then bilking them out of everything they have. (Recently there was even a school that taught young women how to do this.) So be coolheaded and find out about a person's background, present circumstances, and true character beneath any "company manners," before giving that person a tumble.

Women especially should be alert to any warning signs of abusiveness. These signs include streams of belittling remarks; insistence on doing everything his way; a disregard of your ideas, wishes, and feelings; bad temper; and a general negative attitude toward people and the world. These guys are bad bets anyway. Also, walk away from anyone with a real alcohol addiction or other dependency. Don't "take in strays"; you won't reform them—you'll just be their next codependent.

Be wary of using personals columns; there is usually no screening whatsoever of the people who place these ads. It's true that many mature people have found adventures, even true love, through such contacts. Yet a few have been assaulted and murdered, and others have been exposed to bizarre and unpleasant incidents with people who seemed to be from the Twilight Zone. If you do use the personals, have responses sent to the column's blind post office box; and meet at least for the first couple of times in a secure public place. Never openly advertise your address or phone number. (Anyone with access to your city's *Cross-Street Reference* can get your address from your phone number.) Most people who advertise in personals columns or through dating services are neither kooks nor crooks, but a dangerous minority of them are.

The older you get, the more important a prenuptial agreement is—even if you don't marry. Older persons may be romantically less vulnerable than the young, but they usually have more worldly goods and complicated family situations. The questions below may seem like cold water on a torrid love, but some things must be considered, and many other people may be affected. Here are some questions to consider:

- What properties will be joint and what will remain individual?
- Will you have responsibility for each other's debts?
- What are the inheritance wishes when one partner dies?
- Are there pension arrangements to make?

Here are two additional considerations to keep in mind. There may be "palimony" laws in your state that, even if you don't marry, go into effect if you don't have a legal agreement. If you do marry, the agreement must be *pre*nuptial; otherwise state marriage laws will supersede it. Second, there may be a falling out or an illness arising after a while, so it is well to have such issues settled beforehand. It wouldn't hurt to see an attorney on these issues. If all goes well, fine and dandy; if it doesn't, you are covered.

#56

Avoiding Assault and Battery

Lifestyle factors are involved in the majority of assaults. In-depth studies clearly show that certain social habits greatly increase one's likelihood of being an assault and battery victim. Even our idle conversational style can influence our risks. And those of us who stay away from risky occupations, neighborhoods, and pastimes are far safer than the average person. Occasionally bizarre out-of-the-blue assaults on older people do occur, but these are actually rare in most locales. Most potential assaults can be prevented by our own actions.

It's a sad fact that nowadays more than a few people are walking around seething with frustrations and resentments. Touch them wrong and they may fly into a blind, irrational rage. A big percentage of assaults against persons are crimes of impulse and passion. One offender who beat up a senior for not moving his car said, "I got so mad I couldn't see straight." These days, some of the people you run into will also be on drugs.

If possible, always remove yourself from the scene when a sticky situation arises—this is the most reliable way to "win." This is wise whether the other person is a stranger, acquaintance, or family member. If it is a stranger, just leave if you can. If it's someone you know, you might excuse yourself and go to the bathroom for a few minutes, or even feign illness. There's a universal tendency to let sick people off the hook— they aren't considered "fair game."

If someone insults you or is antagonistic, just don't play; don't pick up the gauntlet.

Most of us have deeply ingrained interpersonal habits that are hard to change. Yet how we talk either increases or decreases our risks of violence. Good manners have saved many lives. The main reason offenders give for committing crimes against older people is the profit motive. But when violence was also involved, "they had it coming" reprisals are often reported. There are many cases where a smart remark or a stinging putdown sent someone to the hospital. When you taunt or belittle others, they *will* take it personally.

Be literally dis-arming. The Golden Rule, some form of which exists in all major religions, is excellent crime-avoidance advice. Say whatever you want or need to, but consider how you say it. Say no diplomatically; disagree without adding any rancor; use "I" statements instead of "you" statements, such as "I'd sure like to go out to dinner" rather than "You never go out to dinner with me." "I" statements are nonthreatening, while "you" messages usually come across as accusatory, even when not so intended.

It's foolish to make enemies needlessly; there's enough ill will in the world already.

#57

Family Violence

According to Bureau of Justice statistics, battery is the leading cause of injury among women of all ages, and older men are sometimes victimized too. Often the abuse or violence is perpetrated by spouses, children, or designated caregivers. Although the abuse may be a one-time "act of passion," it is usually a chronic pattern. And, if there is physical abuse, there is virtually always also extensive emotional abuse, which can be even more devastating. (Such abuses sometimes also go hand-in-hand with financial ripoffs of seniors.)

The signs of elder abuse are similar to child and wife abuse: visible injuries, depressed withdrawal and close-mouthedness, dependency, resignation, and low self-esteem. There is often a cover-up and denial to the outside world.

It is an almost universal pattern for abusers to (1) socially isolate and (2) intimidate their victims so that they remain relatively helpless and even active participants in a conspiracy of silence about the abuse. This often makes it extremely difficult for other relatives, social agencies, or the police to intervene effectively.

The best first step for an abused person is to communicate with someone about it. Women's centers across the world have an outstanding record for helping women of all ages disentangle themselves from such situations. The abused can get some of it off her chest, receive immediate emotional support, and see her options more clearheadedly. If you know about an abused person, these are also good people to talk with because of their experience and knowledge. More and more such centers are also extending aid to men.

The evidence clearly shows that abuse patterns almost never get better on their own; they get worse. Outside intervention has proven to be the only reliable remedy. The abused person has to be helped to "go public" with the situation. Often the victim has become so thoroughly fearful and demoralized that outside support and guidance is crucial.

Family violence workers have come to think of abused persons as hostages, entangled in a web of complex emotions and dependencies and in need of rescue. The abuser often doesn't even realize how far off the rails he or she has gotten, which is why outside intervention is so often the only thing that will break the cycle.

If you are being abused, realize you can escape this situation, as hundreds of thousands of others have. First step: Get some outside communication going. If you know of someone being abused, don't close your eyes. Intervene, by calling the police and local social agencies if necessary. If you realize you are an abuser, get help before you do more damage. The good news is that family abuse can be stopped.

#58

Murder—Not Likely

The "average" risk of being murdered this year is less than one in ten thousand, according to FBI statistics. If you stay off mean streets, if you don't sell drugs or join in gang wars or go around with a chip on your shoulder, your chances may drop to one in a million. Although murder is one of the leading causes of death among young males with crime-prone lifestyles, it is quite rare among older people. And you can virtually eliminate the risks if you:

- Follow the tips on home security and going out safely presented in earlier sections.
- Stay away from high-crime districts.
- Don't resist or argue with a robber.
- Don't create needless ill will with others by your words and deeds.
- If you are experiencing domestic troubles or long-standing feuds with acquaintances, do something to cool the situation off. Call a hotline; join a support group; get some outside arbitration.

Research conducted by noted criminologist Marvin Wolfgang and others clearly shows that the majority of murder victims were related to or knew their murderers and that emotional flare-ups or chronic bad feelings were usually involved. In many cases, for example, when a wife kills a husband, the victim was actually the first to become aggressive.

There's a lot to say for getting along.

#59

Dealing with Age Discrimination

There are now many federal and state laws making it a crime to discriminate against someone on the basis of age. As one prime example, federal law prohibits job discrimination toward anyone forty and older, and the Equal Employment Opportunity Commission has been set up to (sort of) enforce it.

Despite the laws, age discrimination is far from over and done with. Unfair distinctions based on age can come in many forms, sometimes out front, sometimes subtle and hard to prove—except that *you know it happened.*

Aside from its personal unpleasantness, age discrimination often leads to second-class treatment or even criminal exploitation and neglect. Don't stand for it.

The two big sources of age discrimination are the lingering false myths detailed in entry #1 and economics. Older workers are often near the top of the wage scale so companies find it profitable to lay them off or pressure them into early retirement, and then they hire cheaper young workers. Older workers can usually be replaced at half the cost or less. Psychologists have also found that some people are just prejudiced against people, including seniors, who are different from themselves. One study even found such people to be prejudiced against a made-up nonexistent group, the "Nacirema"—"American" spelled backwards.

If you encounter interpersonal discrimination, a good first step is to, without rancor, call the person on it. Say something like "Do you dislike older people?" or "Please treat me with consideration and respect." Some clerks, public officials, nurses, or doctors will realize what they're doing and change their ways as a result. But some won't. If the treatment persists, go somewhere else if possible, where you are more welcome and wanted. You might consider sending a letter to the company or clinic telling them why you're leaving. Or you could consult with the offending person's manager. Decent treatment is your birthright.

In any conflict involving discrimination, it is very important to get and retain all the hard evidence you can, including any witnesses. If you have evidence, you will often get fairer treatment without having to go further. Without evidence, it too often ends up being your word against someone else's.

If you feel you have been the victim of job discrimination, contact the nearest Equal Employment Opportunity Office or your country's equivalent. It is important to do this within 180 days, which is the filing limit. Consider retaining a lawyer experienced in handling these cases; your local senior center or aging agency can probably help you.

#60

Recovering from Crime Victimization

Being victimized by any type of crime is usually traumatic. What is important is to get over it as speedily and fully as possible and get on with living. No one has all the answers for getting over such incidents, but here are some pointers from crisis centers and support organizations that have helped many people.

Be thankful for what *didn't* happen. In most crime incidents there are things to be thankful for—it could have been worse. Be thankful if no one was hurt or that you still have your life and freedom, or whatever.

Keep up your exercise and nutrition, even if you don't feel like it. Dropping them can artificially exaggerate post-trauma symptoms and negative feelings.

Don't deny or bury your feelings; let them out. If they remain bottled up, they'll just keep the incident alive and cause other mischief. Some people have written out their feelings—anger, grief, fear—in a journal, and there is evidence that this can be as effective a catharsis as going to a therapist.

Get support. Emotionally supportive friends or family

members who listen appreciatively without just telling you what to think or do are a godsend. There are now also many support groups such as the Older Women's League (OWL) that can be the most valuable factor in recovery. Support groups are growing rapidly in all spheres of life because they have proven so effective. They combine pooled experience and shared strategies for coping, plus caring, listening, and nonjudgmental emotional support. Scientific research has shown that group members have higher levels of immune system cells than nonmembers under similar situations. Even terminally ill patients who join support groups live almost twice as long on the average as those who don't.

Realize there is usually a healing process after crime victimization, just as after an operation or loss of a loved one. Victimization—even the theft of a few dollars or a cheap watch—is a kind of psychological rape. So don't fight the healing process or deny it; honor it, and let it run its course so that you can come out the other side. Also, pamper yourself through the process as you would through a physical injury recovery.

Victim assistance and victim compensation are available in some areas; your network, local social agencies, and Area Agency on Aging can help you secure these. If you will be involved in court proceedings, at a minimum have someone accompany you; judicial systems are not always user-friendly. If you are going to be a witness, ask that any prosecuting attorney provide you with real help. This help should include transportation, coaching, an escort through the process, and any needed protection.

Take measures to prevent a recurrence of the crime. Learn more tricks of crime avoidance and make lifestyle changes accordingly.

If you feel so inclined, join organizations to help others similarly victimized or support programs that help prevent similar occurrences. Many of the best volunteer workers come from the ranks of those who've themselves been victimized. They know what they're talking about—they've been there.

If a loved one has been victimized, be a patient friend for them. Listen to them respectfully (they may keep repeating themselves), give them the aid they desire, let them decide what to do, even if you'd do it differently.

There are second chances, and even third and fourth. This is not an empty pep talk; growing numbers of older people are proving it in their own lives. Don't think victim; think survivor.

Safeguarding Elderly Parents and Relatives

A rapidly growing number of people are now part of the "sandwich generation"—older people who have both adult children and more elderly parents still living. Many older people also have spouses, relatives, or friends who may depend on them to some extent.

So most seniors have other older people they are involved with and care about. And our concern for their well-being and security is natural; if they are hurt, we are hurt.

Being a senior involved in some degree of caregiving for other seniors raises issues, both practical and of the heart, which go far beyond this book. In this chapter we focus on some ways to help everyone concerned remain crime-free.

#61

Secure Living Arrangements

There are essentially five kinds of living arrangements for
your elderly parents and relatives: (1) alone and distant from
their children, (2) alone but near their children, (3) living
with their children, (4) in a retirement complex with some
professional care available, and (5) in a nursing home. The
overwhelming preference among older parents is to live near,
but not with, their kids. The main reason given is that their
own continuing independence is their most valued possession.

Each of these five living patterns presents some security
situations. But again, a few pointers can make all the
difference. A main security problem is that older parents
grew up in a time when you could leave your doors unlocked
and bicycles out in the front yard, when you could stroll
through the streets in the evening by yourself and trust almost
anyone who was nice to you. Most older people know intellec-
tually that these things are no longer true, but deeply
ingrained habits can persist. *One's habits are what really
count in crime prevention.* When I have looked through
victimization cases involving the elderly, I've found the most

common mistake was that they did not take the current crime scene seriously enough. Ironically, the reverse situation also sometimes arises when older persons have been intimidated by exaggerated media coverage or a personal incident to the point that they're afraid to step outside their door.

So what can you do? As caregiving expert E. Jane Hall has pointed out, you can't just "take charge"—your elderly parents are entitled to live their lives as they please, even if it doesn't please you. But you can do quite a bit, really.

Whatever the situation, the help you can give older parents rests on the underpinnings of open communication and listening (which the National Study of Family Strengths found to be the number one trait distinguishing healthy families). Ideally, all parties must feel free to express problems, emotions, and fears, and know they won't be punished in any way. Otherwise, problems are too likely to get hidden away where they fester and aren't dealt with until a real crisis erupts. The final suggestion in the best-selling *Life's Little Instruction Book* is "Call your mother," which is excellent advice—crime-wise and otherwise.

When the older people are geographically distant, helping them remain secure can be a bit tricky, but all major phone carriers now have discount programs where you can stay in frequent touch for under twenty dollars a month. And providing just one or two thwarting measures can really lower their risks.

Don't lecture; wait for what family experts call a "teachable moment"—when the subject of crime and security comes up. Then mention a couple of bottom-line security tips. Suggest what they might do rather than what is scary. You could also bring up security in a general conversational way and proceed from there. Don't be pushy, but offer help. You can send them clippings, not of horror stories but of good tips and successful actions. You can send them a shriek alarm or a copy of this book. In most areas there is now also a call-a-day service available from local senior centers or social agencies. Someone calls elders living alone each day to chat for a moment and see that they are okay. If you visit them, you might see about upgrading their dwelling's security and show them good security habits by your own example. *Anything you do is better than nothing.*

If you have elderly relatives living in another state, there is now a toll-free help service, Eldercare Locator, (800)677-1116. When you call, give the name, address, zip code, and a brief description of the problem, and they will steer you to an appropriate agency or resource. They operate Monday through Friday, 9 A.M. to 6 P.M., eastern standard time.

If the older people live nearby, you can apply the previous suggestions plus many more. With a bit of effort you can extend the umbrella of your own network of allies over them and share in theirs, so that security is mutually increased. You can also share shopping and other errands, which makes both of you safer.

With their agreement, you can help arrange a police security survey of their residence and help them handle any weaknesses; most dwellings can be upgraded with little cost. You can keep an eye on their place if they go on a trip. You can share scam and consumer fraud alerts. You can share reliable repair people and professionals. You can help them connect with resources, such as senior centers, the local AARP chapter and services, and Meals on Wheels, that will both enhance their security and enrich their lives. You can develop a mutual aid relationship where everyone wins but the bad guys.

For economic or health reasons, you and older parents may decide to live together. Families moving back together is now a minitrend. Census data shows that four out of five seniors who are frail or ill are cared for directly by family and friends. With respect to crime, living together has both pluses and minuses. Two or more are safer than one and the increased activity around the dwelling is a good crime deterrent. But the carelessness of others can put you at greater risk. For this reason, it is vital to have a full understanding about maintaining basic security measures, such as always locking up. An excellent book on the venture of living together is *Under One Roof* by Sheelagh McGurn.

If an older parent goes to live in a senior complex, security is usually pretty good, but don't assume this without checking. Security in a senior complex can often be even further upgraded by following the security tips in chapter 2. And do a full investigation of the real costs of living in a complex you are considering. Dig past the promotional come-ons to find out about monthly fees, refund policies, extra charges, and so on. Some of these complexes are ripoffs, but some are very good deals.

#62

Nursing Home Security

The time may come when an older parent needs the care of a nursing home. Despite media horror stories, the majority of these establishments are well-run and caring places that provide a decent quality of life. Yet a nursing home must be chosen with care, and you'll want to maintain a "friendly surveillance" guardianship while the person is there.

Before settling on the nursing home option, check into the alternative of part-time professional home care. More and more state agencies are turning to this alternative because it can be both far cheaper and more in line with the older person's wishes. A visiting nurse, some domestic help, and an emergency medical alert system can give the elderly the help they need while they can still stay in their own residence, surrounded with their own things.

If a nursing home is the best option, and your state has licensing requirements, see that the one you choose is properly certified. This is no guarantee, but it helps eliminate the worst places. A site visit is also crucial. You'll have lots of questions about the care given and facilities. But also, be sensitive to how the place *feels*. Is the atmosphere cheerful or ominous? This may be the best clue to freedom from exploitation.

Consumer advocate groups have set nursing home Patients' Rights standards which militate against abuse. These include privacy; confidential telephone calls; opening one's own mail; freedom from verbal, emotional, or physical abuse; conjugal rights; protection from financial exploitation; protection from overdrugging; and good, sanitary conditions. Breach of these should be considered a crime.

In a nursing home situation, there are several things to beware of:

- Billing frauds, unnecessary referrals, services charged but never rendered.
- Embezzling patients' assets or theft of personal property.
- Employing inadequate or unqualified staff in violation of licensing rules.
- Chronic patterns of neglect of the residents.
- "Pacification"—the overuse of medication to keep patients quiet and tractable, so they are not "bothersome" to the staff. (Patients' symptoms may result from drug pacification more than aging; any age group would show similar signs if similarly medicated.)

You cannot depend on overstretched regulatory agencies to safeguard your loved ones in nursing homes. If you discover a situation, contact the institution's manager first; then if the abuse is not handled satisfactorily, contact the nearest health service agency office, and finally, if necessary, your state attorney general.

Any nursing home resident or concerned relative or friend

can also contact the local ombudsman. Ombudsmen's services are free, they are independent, and they have broad powers of investigation and arbitration. Nursing homes are required to post notices telling how and where to reach them.

Experienced social agency workers have found that an actively and continually caring family member is the best protection a nursing home patient has.

#63

Protecting the Elderly from Exploitation and Abuse

Current research has shown that most people continue to change throughout their entire lifespans, so don't be amazed if your parents or spouse does so. But in some cases these changes are in the direction of increasing frailty, confusion, and suggestibility.

If they become disoriented, the very elderly are sometimes the victims of petty or grand exploitation. Tree trimmers and repair mechanics may overcharge them; home aid workers may steal from them; professionals and tradespeople may send them outrageous bills; unscrupulous promoters may get them to sign over their accounts or properties; some relatives may even descend like vultures to fleece them. Such ploys are especially likely if the elderly are debilitated with illness. You'll need to strike a balance between protecting them and interfering with their lives. Two guidelines: (1) Leave them as much independence as possible and (2) if they're being exploited or abused, go for the throat.

Again, the importance of continual open communication comes into play. The better your communication line, the earlier and more likely you are to learn of any misdeeds, while remedial action can still be taken. Isolation from you aids and abets any malefactor.

Call up the offending party or company and demand decent treatment and a settlement. Hint loudly that if the matter isn't handled satisfactorily, further action will be taken. Don't hesitate to be threatening. (The authorities and judicial system tend to be sympathetic toward the elderly.)

Don't forget the small claims court option for less costly ripoffs. If the situation is more serious or complicated, your best bet would be an attorney specializing in elder law. Honor the older person as someone in recovery from the incident. And, with their cooperation, take steps to prevent a recurrence.

#64

The Right to Live and the Right to Die

Okay—an unpleasant subject.

Things may sail along smoothly for years, even decades, but eventually your older parents and you will face some life-and-death issues. Prior to this, there may be a period of debilitation. For both humane and crime reasons, these issues should be discussed with clearheaded compassion and respect beforehand. If you wait until stressful emergencies arise, all parties involved will be more vulnerable.

The issues surrounding death are not a favorite subject for most people. Yet getting a clear notion of the loved one's wishes, investigating alternatives, comparison shopping, and preplanning accomplish two important things. First, the person's desires will be honored, which can ease everyone's mind. Second, this groundwork helps prevent exploitation at the time of demise or terminal illness. (There is also evidence that such planning can take some of the anguish out of the event.)

It is important to keep in mind that regulations involving wills, estates, and funeral arrangements vary widely from state to state. If the person moves to a different state, different regulations may be in force.

Death can occur unexpectedly, so it's wise to have the following in place:

- Be sure the person has made a will stating his or her wishes for the disposition of belongings and monies. Without a will, the state apportions the estate. A clear will also helps prevent expensive squabbling among the heirs, where lawyers sometimes end up the only ones enriched. You might also want to get together with an attorney who specializes in elder law to set up a living trust, which bypasses most inheritance regulations.
- Find out if the person wants to enact a living will. Modern high-tech medicine can now keep someone less than half alive almost indefinitely. Artificial life-support systems often prolong people's deaths, not their lives. In the process, the person's estate and the family are too often pauperized. If the person wishes to be disconnected, get the proper forms made out and to hand.
- If the person has a lingering terminal illness, consider the hospice alternative, where the person remains at home, is made comfortable, and is given a wide range of support. This can be easier and more secure for all involved. In the United States the number for the National Hospice Organization helpline is (800)658-8898.
- Find out the person's own wishes regarding funeral arrangements beforehand to lessen trauma and needless expense. A growing number of elderly are opting for simple funerals or cremations, so that more of their resources are passed on to the heirs. Many funeral homes are caring and trustworthy, but some are flatly unscrupulous or high-pressure grasping, so it is wise to explore desires and costs in advance. If you'll be footing

the bill, consider spending the money on the person while they're still alive, rather than on an elaborate funeral.

There is a strong tendency for people to shy away from these life and death issues—understandably. But if they are faced and settled they can be put aside, and you can concentrate on enjoying the rewards of the ongoing living relationships.

#65
How to Get Help

It sometimes seems as if the criminals get all the breaks and we are left on our own to deal with their menace. Yet there is a tremendous amount of help available to us and our elderly parents and relatives. But in most cases it is not automatic, and we need to (1) find it and (2) reach out and contact it. I've also found that a bit of perseverance is necessary; the quality of help varies greatly from agency to agency and even from person to person within the same agency. Also, lines are often busy and you have to persist a bit in order to reach someone. On the other hand, I've discovered a wonderful "hidden resource"—people who can help you find help (person A puts you in touch with person B).

The following people and agencies have usually proven able to connect seniors with the help they need: any local senior center, the nearest Area Agency on Aging, the crime prevention unit of your local police department, the local AARP chapter, the local United Way office, your reference librarian (I have found librarians to be awesomely resourceful in finding things out; if there are several area branches, call the main one). In contacting any of these people, state your problem and ask them to tell you who to contact. Sometimes they won't know but they will know who to put you in touch with to find out.

Local newspapers and magazines sometimes publish lists of names and phone numbers of area resources; it's wise to snag these and keep them handy. One problem is that such lists often mix true nonprofit help sources with for-profit institutions and referral services, so this needs to be checked out. From time to time, news articles and even the Dear Abby column will carry information about help resources. Just clip these and add them to your file.

As mentioned previously, the most effective approach is to pool information on help resources with your neighborhood protection network. It's good to have these lists on hand before a problem arises. Perhaps you'll never need them, yet they are still good to have to share with others who run into problems.

There are three levels of help resources: local, state or regional, and national. Local resources are generally the most useful by far—after all, we *live* locally. Even the relevant state and national agencies usually have local offices. Regulatory agencies, usually state and national, are often the places to appeal to when we are getting nowhere locally. However, even when federally funded, most government assistance and regulation is administered by the individual states, which can vary enormously in the way they operate. More and more state and national organizations are putting in toll-free hotlines and helplines so contacting them is free and easy. And new ones, such as the Medicare Fraud hotline, keep coming on line. (See the Appendix for many of these hotlines.)

Because most sources of help are local and the numbers,

addresses, and even names may vary from place to place, it is necessary to build your own help directory. State and national resources can provide local referrals, general information, and a supportive listening ear. In some cases they are also the place to lodge complaints and information on criminality. Whenever you write them, be sure to enclose a self-addressed stamped envelope (folded up inside your letter). This greatly speeds response.

It's wisest to have two directories: the first a short list of immediate emergency numbers, the second a longer list of other help resources.

The emergency list should be permanently posted by each of your phones for quick reference. The emergency list ought to include police (emergency plus your crime prevention liaison member), fire, paramedic/ambulance, at least two of the most reliable and usually available members of your neighborhood network, any relative you can count on on short notice, your auto club, and your insurance agent. Add to this list as you see fit, but keep it fairly short; other resources can go on your long list. It's good to keep this emergency list in your car at all times too, and at work or when traveling.

There are many other help resources available to seniors in addition to crime protection, so read entry #52, "Claiming Your Share" and collect these, too.

Where Do We Go from Here?

What about the national crime scene? And all the crime prevention programs that have been tried? Do they warrant our support? And are they any help to our own personal security and our future safety? In this final chapter, we'll take a closer look at these questions.

#66

National Crime Prevention Programs

In addition to our personal and neighborhood protection measures, we need to pay some attention to the national and even international crime scene. There are at least two strong reasons for doing this. First, national crime comes down on us, just as national storm fronts or economic trends influence our own daily lives. Second, we're all helping foot the bill. Every time we buy a light bulb or loaf of bread, we pay a hidden crime surcharge. Security systems, guards, and losses from thefts and fraud are all expensive, and the expense is passed on to us. So we pay more wherever we go because of crime. It increases all our insurance premiums. And because of crime, higher taxes currently take over a thousand dollars a year from our pockets.

We hear a constant stream of big proposals for dealing with the nation's crime problems. But the real question is, how much will any of these help protect the average senior from victimization? The answer in most cases is, not too much. Wars on crime have frequently been declared by politicians, but with only minimal success. For instance, despite heroic efforts by law-enforcement officers, we're intercepting no more than 10 percent of the drugs coming into the country. Stiffer sentences seem to have just filled our prisons to overflowing. According to the Sentencing Project, a Washington, DC, research group, our national "get tough" policies have produced no dramatic gains in crime control. Capital punishment stops the executed person from committing further crimes, and might make victims' families feel that justice has been served, but its deterrent effect on others is highly questionable. Some kind of gun licensing makes sense, but any real gun control is far more than a day late and a dollar short because there are already fifty million handguns floating around out there.

Rehabilitating criminals so that they rejoin law-abiding society is a dream that hasn't worked out well. Some culprits do change their ways, and a few programs, such as the Delancey Street Foundation in San Francisco, have been very successful in reforming delinquents and ex-cons. But careful analysis by researcher Robert Mortinson and others has shown that rearrest rates after release are usually about the same, whatever the rehabilitation program, or even if there's no program at all. Both "liberal" and "conservative" crime prevention programs have had only marginal influences on our day-to-day level of security, despite the best efforts of law officers. Perhaps these efforts have helped keep crime from getting totally out of hand.

Yet all the national efforts are not in vain. Some of them work and are worthy of our support.

+ ***Massive education and ad campaigns.*** Recently we have had a roughly 3 percent drop each year in the teen use of illicit drugs, and massive educational campaigns are a main reason. Widespread education has also helped prevent many rapes and alerted many seniors so they were able to avoid becoming scam victims. These campaigns work more slowly than we'd like, but their results are more permanent, so they deserve support. A leader in all these efforts is the National Crime Prevention Council, 733 15th Street, NW, Washington, DC 20006; (202)393-7141.

• *Tracking down the superfelons.* Marvin Wolfgang and subsequent researchers have discovered a major crime fact: Most serious crimes are committed by a very small fraction of offenders. Convicting just one superfelon can prevent as much crime as locking up fifty ordinary lawbreakers. Superfelons are not cool professionals, they are berserkers—incorrigible burglars and muggers who commit hundreds of crimes each year, serial child molesters, rapists, and killers. They usually start their crime life at an early age, which is why it's important to prosecute serious and repeat juvenile offenders as adults. In most cases they are apprehended through tips from private citizens, which is why it's so important for us to report crimes and suspicious circumstances to the authorities.

• *Consumer protection and advocate groups.* These have been doing more to protect us from swindles and corporate crime abuses than anyone else. Usually they've fought uphill battles and sometimes they are the targets of smear campaigns by vested interests. Such consumer groups continue to document criminality and unfair practices and they agitate for the government to do something about them. Without their efforts we'd be far more exploited and unprotected from fraud than we are. So they deserve our active support.

♦ *Nature's way.* Neal Shover, Travis Hirschi, and other researchers have unearthed some good news: Many people outgrow a life of crime as they get older. The old saying, "Once a thief, always a thief," isn't true. As they mature, ex-offenders often establish stable relationships with spouses or have jobs that they don't want to jeopardize. Many say they grew tired of the problems and consequences of criminality and dreaded the possibility of another long jail sentence. It seems that even habitual criminals can mellow as they grow older. This is real reform. So give them a second chance.

Supporting crime prevention education, informing authorities, and joining consumer protection groups probably won't makes us safer tonight or tomorrow morning. But by doing so, in the long run, we'll make a real and lasting contribution to everyone's safety.

#67

Personal Protection Today and Tomorrow

Nobody really knows the ultimate causes of crime, and nobody has the ultimate solution for its prevention. So we can't hold our breath, waiting for some election or magnificent piece of research or wonderful new program to resolve our crime problems.

We do know from a mountain of evidence that *all programs and efforts by the authorities are only subsidiary to our own personal security measures.* The police and regulatory officials can never be everywhere at once—and I don't think we'd like a society where they were.

The first, most vital line of defense against crime is our own preventive actions.

The second line consists of the concerted thwarting actions of citizens banding together at the neighborhood and community level.

The third line is our liaison with local police and the higher-up agencies they work with.

The fourth line is the activity of state and national agencies and political leaders. This is least important to our personal daily security.

Nobody knows for sure what the future holds in store. This fact brings to my mind that old Chinese curse: "May you live in interesting times." We *can* say that the threat of crime is not going to disappear from our lives any time soon. And new times will mean new crimes. We'll need to keep up our personal security habits all the days of our lives. Yet the crime protection basics presented in this book will remain effective to help keep you safe, whatever the future brings.

Appendix: Where to Get Help

The following list of suggestions for getting assistance with specific problems isn't exhaustive, and you and your network can easily improve on it. The lion's share of assistance is administered at the local and state levels because this is how benefits are mandated by the federal government's Older Americans Act and its amendments. Some good resources do exist at the national level, and I've listed them. For help with situations not covered here, start with your local senior center or Area Agency on Aging, or try the Yellow Pages under "Senior Citizens' Service Organizations." National references are for the United States but there are comparable resources in almost all industrialized countries.

ABUSE

These cases are often emotionally and legally complicated so it's important to work with a person who has plenty of experience. Seek until you find one. Contact your local Area Agency on Aging and your local women's center. Also contact the excellent National Coalition Against Domestic Violence,

Box 15127, Washington, DC 20003; hotline: (800)333-SAFE.

AGE DISCRIMINATION

For most discrimination situations, ask your local Area Agency on Aging to refer you to a mediation service. These have been successful in four out of five situations in which both parties agree to mediation. For legal recourse in employment discrimination, contact the local Equal Employment Opportunity Commission office or call the national hotline: (800)USA-EEOC.

ALCOHOL PROBLEMS

We've seen that frequent intoxication greatly increases the likelihood of victimization. Medical alcoholism programs are sometimes effective but quite expensive. The Alcoholics Anonymous programs are free (but accept donations) and have a good recovery rate. Check for local listings or contact Alcoholics Anonymous, Box 459 Grand Central Station, New York, NY 10163; (212)686-1100. For relatives and friends of persons with alcohol problems, contact the excellent non-profit support program Al-Anon, either your local chapter or Al-Anon, 1372 Broadway, New York, NY 10018; hotline: (800)356-9996.

CHILD ABUSE

If you know of a child who is being abused, an excellent first step is to talk it over with someone at the confidential National Child Abuse Hotline: (800)422-4453.

CONSUMER FRAUD

Presently local district attorneys and state attorneys general are most effective in dealing with the majority of consumer fraud. They'll be listed in the government section of your phone book. You can also contact the Better Business Bureau. For the AARP Consumer Alert, write to 601 E Street, NW, Washington, DC 20049. Better Business Bureaus and the AARP have no enforcement power but can publicize fraud data to forewarn others.

The nonprofit National Consumers League has also set up a toll-free National Fraud Information Center hotline: (800)876-7060. Call to inquire about a suspicious phone or mail solicitation or if you feel you've been swindled.

CREDIT CARD CRIME

If a credit card is lost or stolen or there is an unlawful billing charged to your account, immediately contact the card issuer; most have a toll-free emergency number listed on their monthly statements. This limits your liability. If you suspect theft, contact the police as soon as possible. If you are disputing an item billed to your account, inform your card issuer by phone and in writing; this "freezes" the charge until the dispute is settled. If you've gotten entangled in credit problems, contact the very helpful, nonprofit Consumer Credit Counseling Service. For the nearest office, check your directory or contact the National Foundation for Consumer Credit, 8701 George Avenue, Suite 601, Silver Springs, MD 20910; (301)589-5600.

DRUG ABUSE

Drug abuse is uncommon among older people, but sometimes they are involved with abusers. Call the Drug Abuse Hotline: (800)622-HELP. Drug abuse in your neighborhood increases most other kinds of crime risks. Talk with your network's crime prevention liaison or call the police with details.

FINANCIAL/INVESTMENT FRAUD

This whole area is very poorly regulated. Your best bet is to contact your local or state attorney general's office. You can also contact the Securities and Exchange Commission, 26 Federal Plaza, Room 1102, New York, NY 10007; (212) 264-1636. One important tactic: make a practice of sending your checks through the mail, because the recipient is then subject to tough, fairly well enforced mail fraud laws. Contact your local chief postal inspector, or you can write to Chief Postal Inspector, U.S. Post Office Department, Washington, DC 20260.

INSURANCE FRAUD

There are three rampant types of insurance crimes: fraudulent insurance claims, misleading sales by insurance carriers, and unfair handling of claims by insurance companies. If you find out about fradulent claims, contact the insurance company involved, which will probably vigorously pursue it. In cases of misleading insurance sales or disputes over claim settlements, contact your state's insurance oversight department, which will usually arbitrate the case. If large sums are involved, you may want to get a lawyer specializing in insurance claims or elder law, but thoroughly explore what this might cost before going ahead.

You can also get some information, aid, and referrals from the National Insurance Helpline: (800)924-4242.

LEGAL ASSISTANCE

Low-cost, even free, legal assistance is available but you sometimes have to scrounge to find it. This is an excellent resource for your network to explore before the need arises; otherwise the unwary can get buried in outrageous fees and "incidental" costs. Check with the nearest Legal Aid Society for starters. Also check with the National Senior Citizens' Law Center, 1709 West Eighth Street, Los Angeles, CA 90017, which can often put you in touch with local sources of low-cost legal aid. Your local United Way can be helpful. And keep small claims court in mind, where no lawyer is required (or sometimes even allowed).

MAIL ORDER FRAUD AND PROBLEMS

If problems with a mail order company arise, you can contact the nearest post office and ask them to steer you to the local postal inspector general. If you paid by credit card, inform the card company in writing and ask them not to pay the bill. Also let your area Better Business Bureau and attorney general's office know.

MEDICAL ABUSES

For Medicare or Medicaid fraud or disputes, call the Medicare hotline: (800)368-5779. If you've encountered malpractice at the hands of health professionals, it's best to get professional legal help (see "Legal Assistance"). An excellent group to join for help with any sort of medical fraud is the People's Medical Society; call toll-free for details: (800)624-8773.

NURSING HOME ABUSES AND CRIMES

Contact the local ombudsman (a public official) listed in the government section of your directory. Also contact your state's department of health. In case of a violent crime immediately contact the local police.

PENSION FUND RIPOFFS

For local- and state-level pension fund problems contact your state attorney general's office. For pensions overseen by the federal government, contact the Pension Guaranty Corporation, 2020 K Street, NW, Suite 700, Washington, DC 20006.

SOCIAL SECURITY–RELATED CRIMES OR PROBLEMS

For any situations involving social security, contact either your local Social Security Administration office or the national helpline: (800)234-5772.

TELEPHONE FRAUD

AT&T customers should call (800)222-0300 (ext. 273); others should call their long-distance companies.

VICTIM ASSISTANCE AND COMPENSATION

If you've been victimized, after informing the authorities, probably the best places to start looking for assistance are your network and police crime prevention liaison. The assistance available depends on the type of crime, but your local senior center and United Way can usually help. If the culprit is to be prosecuted, be certain to get help in wending your way through the judicial system. For immediate support, assistance, and referrals call the Victim Services Hotline: (213)577-7777, or the National Organization for Victim Assistance: (202)232-6682. Many states now have victim financial compensation programs; to inquire, check with your local Area Agency on Aging.

Selected Bibliography

Arluke, Arnold, and Jack Levine. "Another Stereotype: Old Age as a Second Childhood." *Aging* (August 1984): 7–41.

Breckler, Rosemary. *If You're Over 50: You Are the Target.* San Leandro, CA: Bristol, 1991.

Brillon, Yves. *Victimization and Fear of Crime Among the Elderly.* Toronto: Butterworth, 1987.

Budish, Amy and Armond. *Golden Opportunities.* New York: Henry Holt, 1993.

Castleman, Michael. *Crime Free.* New York: Simon & Schuster, 1984.

Cheney, Walter, William Diehm, and Frank Seeley. *The Second 50 Years.* New York: Paragon, 1992.

Conklin, John. *Criminology.* 2d ed. New York: John Wiley, 1986.

Curran, Delores. *Traits of a Healthy Family.* Minneapolis: Winston, 1983.

Dychtwald, Ken. *Age Wave.* Los Angeles: Tarcher, 1989.

Estrella, Manuel, and Martin Forst. *The Family Guide to Crime Prevention.* New York: Beaufort, 1981.

FBI Uniform Crime Report. Washington, DC: U.S. Government Printing Office (published annually).

Felson, Richard, and Henry Steadman. "Situational Factors in Disputes Leading to Criminal Violence." *Criminology* 21 (February 1983): 59–74.

Gottfredson, Michael, and Travis Hirschi. "Why We're Losing the War on Crime." *Washington Post,* September 10, 1989.

Gottlieb, Annie. "Why Older Is Better." *McCall's* (April 1991).

Hall, E. Jane. *Caregiving: How to Care for an Elderly Mother and Stay Sane.* New York: Ballantine, 1990.

Henslin, James M. *Social Problems.* 2d ed. Englewood Cliffs, NJ: Prentice Hall, 1990.

Hills, Stuart L., ed. *Corporate Violence: Injury and Death for Profit*. Totowa, NJ: Rowman & Littlefield, 1987.

Hirschi, Travis, and Michael Gottfredson, eds. *Positive Criminology*. Beverly Hills, CA: Sage, 1987.

Howells, John. *Retirement on a Shoestring*. New York: Gateway, 1992.

Johnson, Ray. "How to Protect Your Home Against Burglars." *U.S. News and World Report* (July 17, 1978): 51–52.

Lipman, Ira. *How to Protect Yourself from Crime*. 3d ed. Chicago: Contemporary Books, 1989.

Macionis, John J. *Sociology*. 3d ed. Englewood Cliffs, NJ: Prentice Hall, 1991.

Maclean, Jack. *Secrets of a Superthief*. New York: Berkley, 1983.

McNamara, Joseph D. *Safe and Sane: The Sensible Way to Protect Yourself, Your Loved Ones, Your Property and Possessions*. New York: Perigee, 1984.

Mokhiber, Russell. *Corporate Crime and Violence*. San Francisco, CA: Sierra Club Books, 1989.

NiCarthy, Ginny. *Getting Free: A Handbook for Women in Abusive Relationships*. Seattle: Seal Press, 1986.

Persico, J. E., and George Sunderland. *Keeping Out of Crime's Way: The Practical Guide for People Over 50*. Glenview, IL: AARP Books, 1985.

Rubington, Earl, and Martin Weinberg. *Deviance: The Interactionist Approach*. 5th ed. New York: Macmillan, 1987.

Schwartz, Joseph. *Don't Ever Retire But Do It Early and Often*. Rockville Center, NY: Farnsworth, 1979.

Siegel, Larry J. *Criminology*. 3d ed. St. Paul, MN: West, 1989.

Simmons, J. L., and George McCall. *76 Ways to Protect Your Child from Crime*. New York: Henry Holt, 1992.

Stokell, Marjorie, and Bonnie Kennedy. *Senior Citizen Handbook*. Englewood Cliffs, NJ: Prentice Hall, 1985.

U.S. Department of Justice. *Sourcebook of Criminal Justice Statistics*. Washington, DC: U.S. Government Printing Office (issued annually).

Veninga, Robert. *Your Renaissance Years*. Boston: Little, Brown, 1991.

Wright, James D. "Second Thoughts About Gun Control." *The Public Interest*, no. 91 (Spring 1988): 23–29.

For background information, I have drawn upon the continuing coverage of crime stories and crime issues in the *Los Angeles Times* and the *St. Louis Post-Dispatch*.